DEDICATION

This book is dedicated to the incredible children who inspire us every day with their boundless curiosity, resilience, and capacity for growth. To the parents, educators, and caregivers who tirelessly nurture and guide them, your unwavering commitment and love lay the foundation for their future. To my own children, whose smiles, questions, and discoveries have been my greatest teachers, thank you for showing me the beauty of each small moment and the importance of patience and kindness. To all the families and educators who strive to make a difference, may this book be a source of support and inspiration as you cultivate positive habits and foster the bright potential within every child.

ϸϸϸ

Contents

Contents

Prayer

"Om Bhadram Karnebhih Shrinuyama Devah

Bhadram Pashyemakshabhiryajatrah

Sthirairangais Tushtuvamsastanubhih

Vyashema Devahitam Yadayuh

Svasti Na Indro Vriddhashravah

Svasti Nah Pusha Vishwavedah

Svasti Nastarkshyo Arishtanemih

Svasti No Brihaspatir Dadhatu

Om Shantih Shantih Shantih"

*This mantra is a prayer for universal well-being, invoking the
blessings of various deities for protection, health, and happiness. It
emphasizes the importance of experiencing the auspicious through all
senses and living a life aligned with divine purpose. The repetition of
"Shantih" at the end signifies a deep desire for peace in the
individual, the environment, and the universe at large. This mantra
is often recited as a prayer for peace, prosperity, and the physical and
spiritual well-being of all beings.*

ppp

About The Author

This book represents the culmination of extensive research and meticulous analysis, incorporating a diverse range of sources, including numerous books, scholarly studies, and personal experiences. Additionally, I have scoured various websites to gather relevant information and data essential for the compilation of this work. I have taken every precaution to ensure the accuracy of the information presented and have diligently cited all sources to acknowledge their contributions.

From her earliest days, Minakshi was distinguished by an insatiable appetite for reading. Her literary universe was inhabited by characters and narratives that spanned ethical tales, motivational and inspirational stories, and the mythic parables imbued with life lessons. This voracious reading habit was not merely for personal edification but was driven by a desire to distill and disseminate the essence of these narratives to foster the development of students and peers alike. She was particularly captivated by the lives and teachings of historical figures and spiritual leaders such as Adi Shankaracharya, Swami Vivekananda, Dr. APJ Abdul Kalam, Mahamana Pandit Madan Mohan Malviya, Mahatma Gandhi, Sardar Vallabhai Patel, and Vinoba Bhave, among others. Their philosophies and life stories fueled her ambition to embody their ideals of resilience, selflessness, and relentless pursuit of knowledge.

Dr. Minakshi's academic and practical engagement with psychology has been equally noteworthy. As a research scholar, her focus has been on exploring the intricate tapestry of the human psyche, aiming to unlock the potential for psychological well-being and societal harmony. Her scholarly work is complemented by her active involvement in social work, where she employs her academic insights to make tangible differences in the lives of the underprivileged. Her endeavours in social work are characterized by an innovative approach that combines traditional wisdom with contemporary psychological practices to address the multifaceted challenges faced by these communities.

Her artistic talents, another facet of her diverse capabilities, are not merely a personal passion but also serve as a medium through which she communicates and connects with others. Her art, rich in symbolism and emotional depth, reflects her philosophical inquiries and social concerns, offering viewers a glimpse into the breadth of her intellect and the depth of her compassion.

In addition to her contributions to the arts and social sciences, Dr. Minakshi has embraced the healing arts of Pranic Healing, mastering the techniques developed by Master Choa Kok Sui. This practice, which focuses on the manipulation of Prana or life energy to heal the body and aura, has been both a personal journey of discovery and a means through which she extends her healing touch to others. Her proficiency in Pranic Healing is complemented by her advocacy and teaching of various forms of meditation aimed at rejuvenation, personal betterment, and the cultivation of harmony within individuals and communities alike.

Dr. Minakshi's life is a narrative of relentless pursuit, not just of personal achievement but of the upliftment and empowerment of society at large. Her diverse interests and talents—spanning the arts, literature, psychology, and the healing practices—converge on a singular path of service. She embodies the spirit of the luminaries who inspired her, channelling their legacy through her actions and teachings. Through her books, art, and social initiatives, she continues to inspire a new generation to embark on their own journeys of self-discovery, resilience, and altruism.

Her commitment to social betterment, particularly her focus on uplifting underprivileged children, reflects a deep understanding of the transformative potential of education and personal development. By integrating her knowledge of psychology, her artistic sensibilities, and her healing practices, Dr. Bansal has developed a holistic approach to social work that addresses both the immediate needs and the long-term well-being of the communities she serves.

As an author, Dr. Minakshi's writings offer a blend of inspirational insights, practical wisdom, and reflective contemplations drawn from her extensive reading and life experiences. Her books serve as a guide for those seeking to navigate the complexities of life with grace, resilience, and purpose. Through her narratives, she extends an invitation to her readers to explore the depths of their own potential and to contribute meaningfully to the collective well-being of society.

In Dr. Minakshi Bansal, we find a remarkable synthesis of the artist, the scholar, the healer, and the social activist. Her life's work stands as a beacon of hope and a source of inspiration for individuals seeking to make a difference in the world. Her story is a compelling reminder of the power of individual action, rooted in compassion and driven by a profound commitment to the betterment of humanity. Dr. Minakshi's legacy is not just in the tangible outcomes of her efforts but in the enduring spirit of inquiry, empathy, and service that she embodies.

ഇഇഇ

Preface

As I embarked on the journey of writing this book, I was driven by a profound belief in the potential of every child to cultivate positive behaviors that will guide them throughout their lives. My experiences as an educator, a mother, and a lifelong learner have shown me the transformative power of habits. Positive habits, once ingrained, become the foundation upon which children can build successful, fulfilling lives. These habits not only shape their daily routines but also influence their mindset, resilience, and overall well-being.

The inspiration for this book came from observing the challenges that many parents and educators face in guiding children towards positive behaviors. In today's fast-paced world, where distractions abound and instant gratification often takes precedence, fostering habits that promote growth, responsibility, and empathy can seem daunting. I wanted to create a resource that would provide practical strategies and insights, grounded in research and real-life experiences, to help children develop the skills they need to thrive.

At the heart of this book is the belief that cultivating positive behaviors is a collaborative effort. It involves parents, educators, caregivers, and, most importantly, the children themselves. By working together, we can create environments that support and nurture the development of beneficial habits. These environments are characterized by consistency, encouragement, and a deep understanding of each child's unique strengths and challenges.

One of the central themes of this book is the importance of mindfulness. Mindfulness is more than just a trendy concept; it is a powerful tool that can help children stay present, manage their emotions, and enhance their focus. By teaching mindfulness practices, we can equip children with techniques to navigate the complexities of their inner and outer worlds. Simple exercises such as deep breathing, body scans, and mindful listening can make a significant difference in a child's ability to handle stress and maintain a calm and centered state of mind.

Another key aspect of fostering positive behaviors is the role of family time. In an era where technology often dominates our attention, dedicating quality time to family activities is crucial. Family time provides opportunities for open communication, shared experiences, and the reinforcement of values. Whether it's through playing games, cooking meals together, or engaging in outdoor adventures, these moments create lasting bonds and instill a sense of belonging and security. Establishing family traditions and rituals further strengthens these connections, providing a framework of continuity and stability.

Gratitude practice is another powerful habit that can significantly impact a child's outlook on life. Teaching children to recognize and express gratitude helps them appreciate the positive aspects of their lives and fosters a sense of contentment. Simple practices like keeping a gratitude journal or sharing daily thankfulness at the dinner table can shift a child's focus from what they lack to what they have. This shift in perspective not only enhances their emotional well-being but also promotes empathy and generosity.

The development of social skills is integral to fostering positive behaviors. Children who can communicate effectively, show empathy, and work cooperatively with others are better equipped to navigate social interactions and build meaningful relationships. Encouraging activities that promote teamwork, such as group projects, sports, and cooperative games, helps children learn the value of collaboration and mutual respect. Role-playing and discussing various social scenarios can also help children develop the skills needed to handle conflicts and build positive connections.

Creative expression is another essential element in the cultivation of positive behaviors. Artistic activities provide children with a unique outlet for self-expression, allowing them to communicate their thoughts and emotions in ways that words may not capture. Whether through drawing, painting, music, or dance, encouraging children to explore their creativity helps them develop critical thinking, problem-solving skills, and emotional intelligence. Creating a supportive environment where artistic expression is valued fosters a sense of confidence and resilience.

Goal setting is a practice that can inspire ambition and achievement. By teaching children how to set and pursue meaningful goals, we help them develop essential skills such as planning, perseverance, and self-discipline. Setting specific, achievable goals and breaking them down into manageable steps makes the process less overwhelming and more attainable. Celebrating small victories along the way reinforces the value of effort and persistence, motivating children to continue striving towards their objectives.

Time management and organizational skills are critical components of effective goal setting. Helping children understand the value of time and teaching them how to prioritize tasks and manage their schedules can significantly enhance their productivity and well-being. Using tools such as planners, calendars, and to-do lists can help children stay organized and focused. Encouraging a balance between responsibilities and leisure activities ensures that children maintain a healthy and fulfilling routine.

Positive self-talk is a powerful tool for building confidence and resilience. Guiding children to use affirming and constructive language when thinking or speaking about themselves can significantly impact their self-esteem and emotional health. Teaching them to recognize and replace negative self-talk with positive affirmations helps them develop a strong sense of self-worth and the ability to cope with challenges. Practicing positive self-talk alongside mindfulness and gratitude reinforces a positive mindset and emotional well-being.

Problem-solving skills are essential for developing critical thinking. Teaching children to approach challenges with a problem-solving mindset involves guiding them through the process of identifying and understanding the problem, generating potential solutions, evaluating and selecting the best option, and implementing and reflecting on the outcome. This approach not only enhances their ability to tackle complex issues but also fosters resilience and adaptability. Encouraging collaborative problem-solving activities and providing opportunities for practical application further enhances these skills.

Habit tracking is an effective method for celebrating progress and fostering personal growth. By monitoring and recording specific actions or behaviors, individuals can gain insights into their habits, maintain motivation, and recognize their accomplishments. Habit tracking encourages consistency and perseverance, reinforcing the importance of incremental progress. Visualizing progress through charts or graphs provides tangible evidence of effort and achievement, boosting motivation and self-efficacy. Celebrating small wins and reflecting on progress fosters a growth mindset and a sense of fulfillment.

Throughout this book, I have drawn on a wealth of research, personal experiences, and insights from experts in various fields. My goal is to provide practical, actionable strategies that can be easily integrated into daily routines. Each chapter offers specific techniques and activities designed to help children develop positive habits and essential life skills. By implementing these practices, parents and educators can create a supportive and nurturing environment that promotes personal growth, emotional well-being, and overall happiness.

In writing this book, I am deeply aware of the diverse challenges that families and educators face. Every child is unique, and there is no one-size-fits-all approach to cultivating positive behaviors. Flexibility, patience, and a willingness to adapt are essential. I encourage readers to tailor the strategies and techniques to suit their individual needs and circumstances. The journey of nurturing positive habits is ongoing, and it requires continuous effort and reflection. However, the rewards are immense, as we help children develop the skills and mindset needed to thrive in all areas of life.

I am grateful for the opportunity to share these insights and strategies with you. My hope is that this book will serve as a valuable resource, providing guidance and inspiration as you support the children in your life. Together, we can create a foundation of positive habits that will empower them to achieve their full potential and lead fulfilling, meaningful lives. Thank you for joining me on this journey, and I look forward to the positive impact we can make together.

Dr. Minakshi Bansal
Social Activist
Ahmedabad, Gujarat, Bharat

ᎮᎮᎮ

ONE

THE FOUNDATION OF POSITIVE HABITS: UNDERSTANDING THE BASICS

The foundation of positive habits lies in understanding the basics of habit formation, which is essential for fostering lasting change in children's behavior. To cultivate positive habits, it's crucial to delve into the science behind habits, the psychology of behavior change, and the practical strategies that make habit formation effective.

Habits are automatic behaviors that are repeated regularly and often unconsciously. They are formed through a process known as habituation, where repeated actions become ingrained in our daily routines. This process is driven by the brain's ability to create neural pathways that make these actions more efficient over time. Understanding this mechanism is key to recognizing why habits are so powerful and how they can be harnessed to promote positive behaviors in children.

The formation of habits involves a cycle known as the habit loop, which consists of three components: the cue, the routine, and the reward. The cue is a trigger that initiates the behavior, the routine is the behavior itself, and the reward is the positive outcome that reinforces the behavior. For example, a child might see their school backpack (cue), pack their homework (routine), and receive praise from their teacher (reward). This cycle reinforces the habit of completing homework regularly.

To lay the foundation for positive habits, it is essential to identify and establish effective cues. Cues can be anything that prompts a particular behavior, such as a specific time of day, a location, an emotional state, or the presence of certain objects. By carefully selecting and consistently using cues, parents and educators can help children develop a reliable trigger for the desired behavior. For instance, setting a specific time each day for reading can help a child develop a habit of reading regularly.

Consistency is another critical element in habit formation. Repetition strengthens the neural pathways associated with a behavior, making it more automatic over time. Consistent practice of a behavior, even in small increments, can lead to the establishment of a strong habit. For children, this means that regular, daily practice of positive behaviors, such as brushing teeth, tidying up, or practicing gratitude, is crucial for ingraining these habits into their routines.

In addition to consistency, the rewards associated with habits play a significant role in reinforcing behavior. Rewards provide positive reinforcement, making it more likely that the behavior will be repeated. Rewards do not have to be extravagant; they can be simple acknowledgments, such as verbal praise, a sticker on a chart, or a few extra minutes of playtime. The key is to ensure that the reward is meaningful to the child and directly follows the behavior to create a strong association.

Understanding the psychology of behavior change is also important in the foundation of positive habits. Children are naturally curious and responsive to their environment, which makes them particularly receptive to habit formation. Theories of behavior change, such as operant conditioning and social learning theory, provide valuable insights into how habits are formed and maintained.

Operant conditioning, a concept developed by B.F. Skinner, emphasizes the role of reinforcement and punishment in shaping behavior. Positive reinforcement, where a behavior is followed by a rewarding outcome, increases the likelihood of that behavior being repeated. Negative reinforcement, where a behavior leads to the removal of an unpleasant stimulus, also strengthens behavior. On the other hand, punishment, which introduces an unpleasant outcome following a behavior, can decrease the likelihood of that behavior. For example, rewarding a child with praise for completing their chores (positive reinforcement) can strengthen the habit of doing chores, while taking away screen time for not completing chores (punishment) can decrease the likelihood of the child neglecting their chores.

Social learning theory, developed by Albert Bandura, highlights the importance of observation and imitation in learning new behaviors. Children often learn habits by observing the actions of those around them, particularly their parents, siblings, and peers. Modeling positive behaviors, such as reading, exercising, or demonstrating kindness, provides children with a blueprint for their own behavior. When children see the positive outcomes associated with these behaviors, they are more likely to adopt them themselves.

In addition to understanding the science and psychology of habit formation, it is essential to implement practical strategies that support the development of positive habits in children. One effective strategy is to start small and gradually build upon success. Breaking down larger goals into manageable, achievable steps can make the process of habit formation less overwhelming for children. For example, if the goal is to develop a habit of reading, starting with just a few minutes of reading each day and gradually increasing the time can help the child build confidence and establish the habit more easily.

Creating a supportive environment is also crucial for fostering positive habits. The environment can either facilitate or hinder habit formation. For children, this means having a structured and predictable routine, as well as access to the tools and resources needed to support the desired behavior. For instance, having a designated reading area with a variety of age-appropriate books can encourage a child to read regularly. Similarly, having healthy snacks readily available can promote healthy eating habits.

Parental involvement and support play a significant role in the development of positive habits in children. Parents can provide guidance, encouragement, and reinforcement to help children stay on track with their habits. Setting clear expectations, providing consistent feedback, and celebrating successes, no matter how small, can motivate children to continue practicing positive behaviors. Additionally, involving children in the process of setting goals and developing habits can give them a sense of ownership and empowerment, increasing their motivation and commitment.

Another important aspect of habit formation is patience and persistence. Developing positive habits takes time and effort, and it is natural to encounter setbacks along the way. It is important for both parents and children to understand that setbacks are a normal part of the process and not a reason to give up. Encouraging a growth mindset, where children view challenges as opportunities for learning and growth, can help them stay resilient and persistent in their efforts to develop positive habits.

Mindfulness and self-awareness are also valuable tools in the foundation of positive habits. Teaching children to be mindful of their actions and the impact of their behaviors can help them make more intentional choices. Mindfulness practices, such as deep breathing, meditation, or reflective journaling, can enhance self-awareness and self-regulation, making it easier for children to stay focused and committed to their habits.

Finally, it is important to recognize that every child is unique, and what works for one child may not work for another. Personalizing the approach to habit formation based on the child's individual needs, preferences, and strengths can increase the likelihood of success. Flexibility and adaptability are key, as parents and educators may need to experiment with different strategies and adjust their approach based on the child's progress and feedback.

In summary, the foundation of positive habits in children is built on a comprehensive understanding of the science and psychology of habit formation, as well as the implementation of practical strategies that support consistency, reinforcement, and a supportive environment. By identifying effective cues, providing meaningful rewards, modeling positive behaviors, and creating a structured and encouraging environment, parents and educators can help children develop lasting positive habits. Patience, persistence, mindfulness, and personalization are essential components of this process, ensuring that children are equipped with the skills and mindset needed to cultivate positive behaviors and thrive in their daily lives.

ppp

"Positive habits are the seeds we plant today to harvest a future of growth and fulfillment. Consistency in these habits nurtures resilience and confidence. Celebrate every small step forward, for each one builds a path to success."

TWO

ROUTINE BUILDING: THE POWER OF CONSISTENCY

Routine building and the power of consistency play a pivotal role in shaping children's behaviors and habits, providing them with a sense of stability, structure, and predictability. Establishing routines is essential for fostering positive behaviors, enhancing time management, and creating a nurturing environment that supports overall development. By understanding the importance of consistency and implementing effective strategies, parents and educators can help children develop healthy, productive routines that contribute to their growth and well-being.

Consistency is the cornerstone of routine building. It refers to the regularity and reliability of actions, creating a predictable pattern that children can rely on. When children experience consistency in their daily lives, they feel more secure and confident, knowing what to expect and how to navigate their environment. This sense of stability is particularly important for young children, who thrive on routine and predictability.

Routines help children develop a sense of time management and organization. By following a structured schedule, children learn to allocate their time effectively, balancing various activities such as schoolwork, play, chores, and rest. This skill is crucial for their academic success and overall productivity. A well-established routine can also reduce stress and anxiety, as children know what tasks need to be completed and when, allowing them to focus on each activity without feeling overwhelmed.

Morning routines are a prime example of how consistency can set the tone for the entire day. A consistent morning routine helps children start their day with a sense of purpose and readiness. Activities such as waking up at the same time, brushing teeth, having a nutritious breakfast, and getting dressed for school become ingrained habits that promote a positive and productive start to the day. When these activities are performed consistently, children are more likely to be punctual, prepared, and focused, enhancing their overall performance and well-being.

Bedtime routines are equally important in promoting healthy sleep habits and ensuring that children get adequate rest. A consistent bedtime routine helps signal to the body that it is time to wind down and prepare for sleep. Activities such as taking a bath, reading a book, and practicing relaxation techniques can create a calming environment that facilitates a smooth transition to sleep. Consistent sleep patterns contribute to better physical and mental health, improved mood, and enhanced cognitive function.

Routines also play a crucial role in promoting healthy eating habits. Establishing regular meal times and involving children in meal preparation can foster a positive relationship with food. When children know that meals are served at consistent times, they are more likely to develop healthy eating patterns and make nutritious choices. Additionally, involving children in meal planning and preparation can teach them valuable skills and encourage them to try new foods, expanding their palate and promoting a balanced diet.

Exercise and physical activity are essential components of a healthy lifestyle, and routines can help incorporate these activities into daily life. Setting aside specific times for physical activity, such as playing sports, going for a walk, or participating in a dance class, can ensure that children get the exercise they need to stay healthy and active. Consistent physical activity routines also promote the development of motor skills, coordination, and overall fitness, contributing to a child's physical and emotional well-being.

Mindfulness and relaxation practices can be integrated into routines to help children manage stress and develop emotional resilience. Activities such as deep breathing, meditation, or practicing gratitude can be included in daily routines to promote mindfulness and self-awareness. Consistency in these practices helps children develop coping strategies and emotional regulation skills, enabling them to navigate challenges and maintain a positive outlook.

Routines are also valuable in fostering academic success and a love for learning. Establishing regular study times and creating a designated homework space can help children develop effective study habits and improve their focus and concentration. Consistent study routines provide structure and discipline, making it easier for children to complete assignments and achieve their academic goals. Additionally, incorporating reading time into daily routines can cultivate a love for books and enhance literacy skills, laying a strong foundation for lifelong learning.

Family routines and traditions play a significant role in strengthening family bonds and creating a sense of belonging. Activities such as family meals, game nights, or weekend outings provide opportunities for meaningful interactions and quality time together. Consistent family routines foster a supportive and nurturing environment, promoting open communication and positive relationships. These shared experiences create lasting memories and reinforce the values and principles that guide a family's dynamics.

Chore routines are an effective way to teach children responsibility and cooperation. Assigning age-appropriate chores and establishing a consistent schedule for completing them helps children understand the importance of contributing to household tasks. Chore routines instill a sense of accountability and teamwork, as children learn to work together to maintain a clean and organized home. Consistent routines also help children develop time management skills and a sense of accomplishment as they complete their assigned tasks.

Incorporating creative activities into routines can encourage artistic expression and foster a love for the arts. Setting aside time for activities such as drawing, painting, playing a musical instrument, or engaging in imaginative play allows children to explore their creativity and develop their artistic talents. Consistent practice of creative activities enhances cognitive development, problem-solving skills, and emotional expression, contributing to a child's overall growth and well-being.

Developing social skills and fostering friendships can also be supported through routines. Scheduling regular playdates, group activities, or family gatherings provides opportunities for children to interact with peers and build social connections. Consistent social routines help children develop communication skills, empathy, and cooperation, which are essential for forming positive relationships and navigating social environments.

Positive reinforcement is an important aspect of routine building. Recognizing and celebrating children's efforts and achievements reinforces the value of consistency and encourages them to maintain their routines. Rewards do not have to be material; verbal praise, a hug, or a simple acknowledgment can go a long way in motivating children to stick to their routines. Consistent positive reinforcement helps children associate their efforts with positive outcomes, making them more likely to continue their productive behaviors.

Flexibility within routines is also important to accommodate changes and unexpected events. While consistency is key, it is essential to recognize that routines should not be rigid or overly restrictive. Allowing for flexibility and adapting routines to suit changing circumstances helps children develop resilience and adaptability. This balance ensures that routines remain effective and sustainable over time, while also providing the necessary structure and stability.

Parents and educators play a crucial role in modeling consistent behaviors and routines. Children learn by observing the actions of those around them, and consistent modeling of positive routines sets a powerful example. Demonstrating the importance of routines through personal practice reinforces their value and encourages children to adopt similar behaviors. Consistent modeling also provides a reference point for children, helping them understand the benefits of routine and consistency.

Communication and collaboration between parents and educators are essential for establishing and maintaining effective routines. Sharing information about a child's routines and progress ensures that both parties are aligned and working towards the same goals. Consistent communication helps identify any challenges or areas for improvement, allowing for timely adjustments and support. This collaborative approach creates a cohesive and supportive environment that promotes the development of positive routines.

Routine building is a gradual process that requires patience, persistence, and continuous reinforcement. It is important to start with small, manageable steps and gradually build upon success. Consistently practicing and reinforcing routines over time helps children internalize these behaviors and make them an integral part of their daily lives. Celebrating progress and milestones along the way reinforces the value of routines and motivates children to continue their efforts.

In conclusion, routine building and the power of consistency are fundamental to fostering positive behaviors and habits in children. By establishing structured routines, providing consistent reinforcement, and modeling positive behaviors, parents and educators can create a supportive environment that promotes stability, organization, and overall well-being. Consistent routines help children develop essential skills, manage their time effectively, and navigate their daily lives with confidence and purpose. The gradual and persistent practice of routines ensures that positive behaviors become ingrained habits, contributing to the long-term success and growth of children. Through patience, flexibility, and collaboration, the power of consistency can be harnessed to create lasting positive change in children's lives.

ppp

"Mindfulness teaches children the power of being present. Through simple practices like deep breathing, they learn to manage emotions and stay focused. This calmness fosters a foundation of emotional strength."

THREE

MORNING HABITS: STARTING THE DAY RIGHT

Morning habits are crucial for setting the tone for the entire day, especially for children. Establishing positive morning habits can foster a sense of routine, discipline, and readiness that prepares children for a productive day. These habits are not just about getting through the morning but about creating a foundation that promotes physical, mental, and emotional well-being. By focusing on key aspects such as wake-up routines, personal hygiene, nutrition, and mindfulness, parents and educators can help children start their day on the right foot.

The first step in creating positive morning habits is establishing a consistent wake-up time. Consistency in waking up at the same time every day helps regulate a child's internal clock, making it easier for them to wake up naturally and feel more rested. This consistency is particularly important for young children, who need regular sleep patterns to support their growth and development. Ensuring that children go to bed at a reasonable hour and get enough sleep is crucial, as it impacts their ability to wake up on time and start the day feeling refreshed.

Once a consistent wake-up time is established, the next step is creating a wake-up routine that eases children into the day. This can include gentle activities such as stretching, deep breathing, or a brief moment of quiet reflection. These activities help children transition from sleep to wakefulness gradually, reducing morning grogginess and promoting a calm start to the day. For younger children, parents can make this routine enjoyable by incorporating playful elements or songs, making it a positive and anticipated part of their morning.

Personal hygiene is another essential component of a positive morning routine. Teaching children to brush their teeth, wash their face, and comb their hair as soon as they wake up instills good hygiene habits that will benefit them throughout their lives. These activities also help children feel more awake and alert, contributing to their overall sense of readiness for the day. Parents can make personal hygiene routines more engaging by turning them into fun rituals, such as using colorful toothbrushes or singing songs while washing up.

Nutrition plays a vital role in a child's ability to start the day right. A healthy, balanced breakfast provides the energy and nutrients needed for physical and cognitive function. Skipping breakfast can lead to decreased concentration, irritability, and fatigue, making it harder for children to focus and perform well in school. Parents should prioritize preparing nutritious breakfasts that include a mix of protein, whole grains, fruits, and vegetables. Involving children in the preparation of their breakfast can also be a fun and educational activity, teaching them about healthy eating and encouraging them to make nutritious choices.

In addition to nutrition, hydration is important for a child's morning routine. Encouraging children to drink a glass of water first thing in the morning can help rehydrate their bodies after a night's sleep and kickstart their metabolism. Parents can make this a habit by placing a water bottle by their child's bedside or in the kitchen, making it easily accessible and a natural part of their morning routine.

Physical activity in the morning can have significant benefits for children. Incorporating exercise into the morning routine, whether it's a quick jog, a few minutes of stretching, or a short yoga session, helps wake up the body and mind. Physical activity releases endorphins, which can improve mood and reduce stress, setting a positive tone for the day. For younger children, making physical activity fun and playful, such as dancing to their favorite songs or playing a quick game of tag, can make it an enjoyable part of their morning.

Mindfulness and relaxation practices can also enhance a child's morning routine. Activities such as deep breathing exercises, meditation, or practicing gratitude can help children start their day with a calm and focused mindset. These practices promote emotional regulation and self-awareness, helping children manage stress and approach their day with a positive attitude. Parents can introduce mindfulness practices gradually, starting with simple exercises and gradually increasing the duration as children become more comfortable with them.

In addition to these key components, organizing the morning routine to minimize stress and chaos is important. Preparing for the day the night before can make mornings smoother and more manageable. This can include tasks such as laying out clothes, packing school bags, and preparing lunches. By doing these activities in advance, children and parents can avoid the morning rush and reduce the likelihood of forgotten items or last-minute stress. Creating a checklist or visual schedule can also help children stay organized and remember their tasks, promoting independence and responsibility.

Positive morning habits also involve fostering a positive and supportive environment. Encouraging words and positive reinforcement from parents can make a significant difference in a child's attitude and motivation. Simple gestures such as a warm greeting, a hug, or words of encouragement can boost a child's confidence and set a positive tone for the day. Creating a pleasant and welcoming atmosphere at home, free from unnecessary distractions or conflicts, can further enhance the effectiveness of morning routines.

Another important aspect of morning habits is fostering a sense of independence and self-sufficiency in children. Encouraging children to take responsibility for their morning routines, such as dressing themselves, preparing their breakfast, or organizing their school materials, promotes autonomy and confidence. Providing age-appropriate tasks and gradually increasing their responsibilities as they grow helps children develop important life skills and a sense of accomplishment. Parents can support this process by offering guidance and assistance when needed, while also allowing children the freedom to learn and practice on their own.

Technology use in the morning should be approached with caution. While educational apps or programs can be beneficial, excessive screen time in the morning can be distracting and counterproductive. It's important to set clear boundaries and limits on screen time, ensuring that it doesn't interfere with essential morning activities such as eating breakfast, getting ready for school, or engaging in physical activity. Encouraging children to focus on more interactive and engaging activities in the morning can help them start the day with a clear and focused mind.

Establishing and maintaining positive morning habits requires consistency and patience. It's important for parents and educators to model these habits and routines, demonstrating their importance and value. Children are more likely to adopt positive behaviors when they see them consistently practiced by the adults around them. Additionally, providing positive reinforcement and celebrating small successes can motivate children to stick to their routines and continue developing positive habits.

It's also important to recognize that morning routines may need to be adjusted and adapted over time. As children grow and their schedules change, their morning routines may need to evolve to accommodate new activities or responsibilities. Flexibility and open communication between parents and children can help ensure that morning routines remain effective and supportive. Regularly checking in with children about their routines and making adjustments as needed can help maintain their engagement and motivation.

Challenges and setbacks are a natural part of developing morning habits, and it's important to approach them with patience and understanding. If a child struggles with certain aspects of their morning routine, it can be helpful to identify the underlying issues and address them collaboratively. For example, if a child has difficulty waking up on time, adjusting their bedtime or creating a more calming bedtime routine may help improve their sleep quality. Encouraging children to share their thoughts and feelings about their routines can also provide valuable insights and help find solutions that work for them.

Incorporating elements of fun and creativity into morning routines can make them more enjoyable and engaging for children. Activities such as playing music, incorporating games, or creating themed mornings can add a sense of excitement and anticipation to the routine. By making mornings a positive and enjoyable experience, children are more likely to look forward to their routines and develop lasting positive habits.

Morning habits are not only about completing tasks but also about fostering a sense of purpose and intention for the day. Encouraging children to set daily goals or intentions can help them approach their day with a clear focus and motivation. This practice can be as simple as asking children what they are looking forward to or what they hope to accomplish each day. Setting positive intentions helps children develop a proactive mindset and a sense of direction, enhancing their overall productivity and well-being.

Parents and educators play a crucial role in supporting children in developing positive morning habits. Providing consistent guidance, encouragement, and support can help children navigate the challenges and successes of establishing routines. By working together and creating a positive and structured environment, parents and educators can help children develop the skills and habits needed to start their day right and thrive in their daily lives.

In summary, morning habits are essential for setting a positive and productive tone for the day. By establishing consistent wake-up times, incorporating personal hygiene, nutrition, physical activity, mindfulness, and organization into morning routines, parents and educators can help children develop habits that promote overall well-being. Creating a supportive and positive environment, fostering independence, and maintaining flexibility and patience are key components of successful morning routines. Through consistent practice and positive reinforcement, children can develop the skills and habits needed to start their day right and achieve their full potential.

ϷϷϷ

"Family time is the heartbeat of strong relationships. Engaging in shared activities creates cherished memories and deepens bonds. These moments of connection provide stability and a sense of belonging."

FOUR

BEDTIME RITUALS: ENDING THE DAY PEACEFULLY

Bedtime rituals are essential for ending the day peacefully and ensuring that children get the rest they need to grow, develop, and function well during the day. Establishing a consistent and calming bedtime routine can have a significant impact on a child's overall health, behavior, and emotional well-being. By focusing on key elements such as a consistent bedtime, relaxing activities, personal hygiene, and creating a conducive sleep environment, parents can help their children develop healthy sleep habits that will benefit them throughout their lives.

One of the most important aspects of a successful bedtime routine is establishing a consistent bedtime. Going to bed at the same time every night helps regulate a child's internal clock, making it easier for them to fall asleep and wake up at the same time each day. Consistency in bedtime is particularly crucial for young children, whose bodies and minds thrive on routine and predictability. Parents can support this by setting a fixed bedtime and sticking to it, even on weekends and holidays. This regularity reinforces the body's natural sleep-wake cycle and helps children feel more rested and alert during the day.

Creating a calm and relaxing atmosphere before bed is essential for helping children wind down and prepare for sleep. Engaging in calming activities in the hour leading up to bedtime can signal to the body that it is time to relax and transition to sleep. These activities can include reading a book, listening to soft music, or engaging in quiet play. Avoiding stimulating activities such as watching television, playing video games, or using electronic devices is crucial, as the blue light emitted by screens can interfere with the production of melatonin, a hormone that regulates sleep. Encouraging children to engage in screen-free activities before bed can promote better sleep quality and make it easier for them to fall asleep.

Personal hygiene is another important component of a bedtime routine. Encouraging children to brush their teeth, wash their face, and take a bath or shower before bed helps establish good hygiene habits and can have a calming effect. The warm water of a bath or shower can relax the muscles and signal to the body that it is time to wind down. Incorporating personal hygiene into the bedtime routine also ensures that these essential tasks are completed consistently, promoting overall health and well-being.

Reading before bed is a time-honored tradition that offers numerous benefits for children. Reading a book or being read to can be a soothing activity that helps children relax and transition to sleep. It also provides an opportunity for parent-child bonding and encourages a love for books and learning. Choosing age-appropriate and calming stories can help create a peaceful bedtime atmosphere. For older children who read independently, providing a variety of books and creating a cozy reading nook can make reading an enjoyable part of their bedtime routine.

In addition to reading, mindfulness and relaxation techniques can be incorporated into the bedtime routine to promote calm and ease the transition to sleep. Activities such as deep breathing exercises, progressive muscle relaxation, or guided imagery can help children release tension and quiet their minds. Practicing gratitude by reflecting on positive experiences from the day can also create a sense of contentment and relaxation. Teaching children these mindfulness practices not only helps them fall asleep more easily but also equips them with valuable tools for managing stress and anxiety.

Creating a sleep-conducive environment is crucial for promoting restful sleep. The bedroom should be a quiet, cool, and dark space that is free from distractions. Investing in comfortable bedding, blackout curtains, and a white noise machine can help create an optimal sleep environment. Keeping the bedroom clutter-free and designating it as a space for sleep and relaxation, rather than play or work, can reinforce the association between the bedroom and sleep. Ensuring that the bedroom is a calm and inviting space can make it easier for children to fall asleep and stay asleep throughout the night.

Establishing a bedtime routine also involves setting clear and consistent expectations for bedtime behavior. Communicating these expectations to children and reinforcing them consistently helps create a sense of structure and security. For example, parents can create a visual schedule or checklist that outlines the steps of the bedtime routine, such as putting on pajamas, brushing teeth, and reading a book. This visual aid can serve as a reminder for children and help them understand and follow the routine independently. Providing positive reinforcement, such as praise or a sticker chart, can motivate children to stick to their bedtime routine and develop good sleep habits.

In addition to the practical aspects of a bedtime routine, emotional support and connection are vital for helping children feel safe and secure at bedtime. Taking a few minutes to talk about the day, share thoughts and feelings, or engage in a comforting bedtime ritual, such as singing a lullaby or giving a goodnight hug, can provide a sense of comfort and reassurance. This emotional connection helps children feel loved and supported, making it easier for them to relax and fall asleep.

For children who have difficulty falling asleep or experience bedtime anxiety, it is important to address these issues with patience and understanding. Identifying the underlying causes of sleep difficulties, such as fears, worries, or changes in routine, can help parents provide appropriate support and interventions. Gradual adjustments to the bedtime routine, such as gradually moving bedtime earlier or incorporating additional calming activities, can help ease the transition to sleep. For persistent sleep issues, seeking guidance from a pediatrician or sleep specialist may be necessary to identify and address any underlying sleep disorders.

Bedtime routines can also be adapted to suit the individual needs and preferences of each child. Some children may benefit from additional sensory input, such as a weighted blanket or a calming scent like lavender, while others may prefer a quiet and minimalist environment. Personalizing the bedtime routine based on the child's unique needs and preferences can make it more effective and enjoyable. Flexibility and willingness to adjust the routine as needed can help ensure that it remains effective and supportive over time.

Parents play a crucial role in modeling healthy sleep habits and routines. Demonstrating the importance of a consistent bedtime, engaging in relaxing activities, and prioritizing personal hygiene sets a positive example for children. When parents practice good sleep habits themselves, it reinforces the value of these routines and encourages children to adopt similar behaviors. Creating a family culture that prioritizes sleep and relaxation can have a lasting impact on children's sleep habits and overall well-being.

It is also important to recognize that establishing and maintaining bedtime routines requires consistency and persistence. Developing healthy sleep habits is a gradual process, and it is natural to encounter challenges and setbacks along the way. Patience and a positive attitude can help children stay motivated and committed to their bedtime routine. Celebrating small successes and providing encouragement can reinforce the importance of the routine and make it a positive and enjoyable experience.

As children grow and their needs change, their bedtime routine may need to be adjusted accordingly. Regularly reviewing and updating the routine to reflect changes in the child's schedule, preferences, and developmental stage can help ensure that it remains effective and supportive. Open communication with children about their bedtime routine and involving them in the process of making adjustments can also promote a sense of ownership and responsibility.

In summary, bedtime rituals are essential for ending the day peacefully and ensuring that children get the rest they need for their overall health and well-being. By establishing a consistent bedtime, engaging in calming activities, prioritizing personal hygiene, creating a sleep-conducive environment, and providing emotional support, parents can help their children develop healthy sleep habits. Consistency, patience, and flexibility are key to maintaining an effective bedtime routine that supports children's growth and development. Through positive reinforcement and modeling healthy sleep habits, parents can create a nurturing environment that promotes restful sleep and a peaceful end to the day.

ppp

"Gratitude transforms the ordinary into extraordinary. Teaching children to appreciate the small joys cultivates a positive outlook. This practice of thankfulness nurtures empathy and happiness."

FIVE

Healthy Eating: Nurturing Nutritious Choices

Healthy eating is a cornerstone of overall well-being and development, particularly for children. Establishing nutritious eating habits early in life can set the stage for a lifetime of good health, supporting physical growth, cognitive development, and emotional stability. Parents and caregivers play a crucial role in nurturing these habits by providing balanced meals, fostering a positive attitude towards food, and creating an environment that encourages healthy eating.

The foundation of healthy eating begins with an understanding of the essential nutrients that children need to grow and thrive. A balanced diet includes a variety of foods that provide carbohydrates, proteins, fats, vitamins, and minerals. Carbohydrates, found in foods such as whole grains, fruits, and vegetables, are the body's primary source of energy. Proteins, present in meat, fish, beans, and nuts, are crucial for growth and tissue repair. Healthy fats, found in avocados, nuts, and olive oil, are essential for brain development and hormone production. Vitamins and minerals, obtained from a diverse range of fruits, vegetables, and whole foods, support various bodily functions and strengthen the immune system.

Creating balanced meals that incorporate these nutrients is vital for children's health. Breakfast, often considered the most important meal of the day, should provide a good mix of carbohydrates, proteins, and healthy fats to fuel the body and brain for the day ahead. A healthy breakfast might include whole-grain cereal with milk and fruit, eggs with whole-grain toast, or yogurt with nuts and berries. Lunch and dinner should also be balanced, including lean proteins, whole grains, and plenty of vegetables. Snacks can be an opportunity to provide additional nutrients and keep energy levels stable throughout the day. Offering fruits, vegetables, nuts, or whole-grain crackers as snacks can help maintain a balanced diet and prevent unhealthy eating habits.

In addition to providing balanced meals, it is essential to foster a positive attitude towards food. This can be achieved by involving children in the process of meal planning and preparation. When children participate in selecting and preparing their meals, they are more likely to develop an interest in and appreciation for healthy foods. This involvement can also be a valuable educational experience, teaching children about nutrition, cooking skills, and the importance of a varied diet. Encouraging children to try new foods and flavors can expand their palate and help them develop a taste for a wide range of nutritious foods.

Creating a positive mealtime environment is another crucial aspect of nurturing healthy eating habits. Mealtimes should be a time for family connection and enjoyment, free from distractions such as television or electronic devices. This focus on the meal and family conversation helps children develop mindful eating habits, paying attention to their hunger and fullness cues and savoring their food. Establishing regular meal and snack times also provides a sense of routine and stability, which can be reassuring for children and help regulate their appetite.

It is important to model healthy eating behaviors as children often imitate the habits of their parents and caregivers. Demonstrating a balanced approach to eating, enjoying a variety of healthy foods, and practicing mindful eating can set a positive example for children. Avoiding restrictive or punitive approaches to food, such as labeling foods as "good" or "bad" or using food as a reward or punishment, can prevent the development of unhealthy attitudes towards food and eating.

Hydration is another key component of a healthy diet. Encouraging children to drink water throughout the day helps maintain hydration, supports bodily functions, and can prevent overeating by distinguishing between thirst and hunger. Sugary drinks, such as soda and fruit juices, should be limited as they can contribute to excessive calorie intake and dental problems. Offering water, milk, or small amounts of 100% fruit juice can help maintain proper hydration and provide essential nutrients.

Addressing picky eating habits is a common challenge for many parents. It is important to approach picky eating with patience and persistence, understanding that it is a normal part of development for many children. Offering a variety of foods without pressure and allowing children to explore new foods at their own pace can help reduce resistance. Creating a positive and relaxed mealtime atmosphere, where children feel comfortable trying new foods without fear of punishment or coercion, can encourage a more adventurous approach to eating.

Education about nutrition and healthy eating can also be integrated into everyday life. Teaching children about the benefits of different foods and how they contribute to their health can empower them to make informed choices. Simple explanations about how fruits and vegetables provide vitamins and minerals, or how protein helps build strong muscles, can make nutrition relatable and understandable for children. Additionally, using fun and engaging activities, such as gardening, cooking classes, or nutrition-themed games, can reinforce these concepts and make learning about healthy eating enjoyable.

School and community programs can also play a significant role in promoting healthy eating habits. Schools can provide nutritious meals and snacks, incorporate nutrition education into the curriculum, and create a supportive environment that encourages healthy choices. Community initiatives, such as farmers' markets, community gardens, and cooking workshops, can provide access to fresh, local produce and opportunities for families to learn about and engage with healthy eating practices.

Addressing and preventing childhood obesity is an important aspect of promoting healthy eating habits. Childhood obesity can have serious health consequences, including an increased risk of chronic diseases such as diabetes, heart disease, and certain cancers. Preventing obesity involves creating a balanced and active lifestyle, which includes regular physical activity and a healthy diet. Encouraging children to be physically active, limiting sedentary behaviors such as screen time, and providing nutritious meals and snacks are key strategies for maintaining a healthy weight. It is important to approach this issue with sensitivity and support, focusing on overall health and well-being rather than weight alone.

For children with dietary restrictions or special nutritional needs, it is important to provide appropriate alternatives and ensure that their dietary requirements are met. This may involve working with healthcare professionals, such as pediatricians or dietitians, to create a balanced and nutritious meal plan that accommodates their needs. Providing a variety of foods and being creative with meal preparation can help ensure that children with dietary restrictions still enjoy a diverse and satisfying diet.

Cultural and familial influences also play a significant role in shaping children's eating habits. Embracing and celebrating cultural food traditions can enrich a child's diet and provide a sense of identity and connection. Incorporating a variety of cultural foods into meals can expose children to different flavors and ingredients, broadening their dietary preferences and fostering an appreciation for diverse cuisines. Family traditions and rituals around food can also strengthen family bonds and create positive associations with healthy eating.

Preventing and addressing food insecurity is a critical aspect of promoting healthy eating habits. Food insecurity, or the lack of consistent access to enough nutritious food, can have detrimental effects on a child's health and development. Ensuring that all children have access to adequate and healthy food is essential for their growth and well-being. Community programs, food assistance initiatives, and policies that support food security can help provide the resources needed to ensure that children receive the nutrition they need.

Creating a balanced approach to treats and indulgences is also important in nurturing healthy eating habits. While it is essential to prioritize nutritious foods, it is also important to allow room for occasional treats and indulgences. Teaching children about moderation and balance can help them develop a healthy relationship with food, where they can enjoy treats without guilt or overindulgence. Creating a positive and balanced approach to treats can prevent the development of restrictive or binge-eating behaviors and promote a healthy and sustainable eating pattern.

It is important to recognize that every child is unique, and their nutritional needs and preferences may vary. Being attuned to a child's individual needs, preferences, and any potential food sensitivities or allergies is crucial for providing appropriate and supportive nutrition. Flexibility and adaptability in meal planning and preparation can help ensure that each child's needs are met while promoting a positive and enjoyable eating experience.

Parents and caregivers play a central role in nurturing healthy eating habits by providing balanced meals, fostering a positive attitude towards food, and creating an environment that encourages healthy choices. Through consistency, education, and positive reinforcement, children can develop the skills and habits needed to make nutritious choices and maintain a healthy diet throughout their lives. Emphasizing the importance of a balanced diet, involving children in meal planning and preparation, and creating a positive mealtime environment are key strategies for promoting healthy eating habits. By addressing challenges such as picky eating, food insecurity, and dietary restrictions with patience and support, parents and caregivers can help children develop a healthy relationship with food and lay the foundation for a lifetime of good health. Through a combination of practical strategies, education, and a supportive environment, healthy eating can become a natural and enjoyable part of a child's daily life, contributing to their overall well-being and development.

ppp

"Effective communication is the cornerstone of social skills. Encouraging open dialogue helps children express themselves clearly and listen with empathy. These skills build meaningful and lasting relationships."

SIX

EXERCISE AND PLAY: PROMOTING PHYSICAL ACTIVITY

Exercise and play are vital components of a child's development, promoting not only physical health but also mental and emotional well-being. Encouraging children to engage in regular physical activity through exercise and play helps build strong muscles and bones, improve cardiovascular health, and develop motor skills. Beyond the physical benefits, active play also fosters social skills, creativity, and cognitive development, making it an essential part of a holistic approach to raising healthy and well-rounded children. To fully appreciate the importance of exercise and play, it is crucial to understand the different forms they can take, the benefits they offer, and the ways parents and caregivers can promote active lifestyles.

Physical activity for children can be broadly categorized into structured exercise and unstructured play. Structured exercise includes organized activities such as sports, dance classes, and physical education programs. These activities provide children with opportunities to learn new skills, work as part of a team, and follow rules and instructions. Organized sports, for example, teach children about discipline, perseverance, and teamwork while providing a fun and engaging way to stay active. Dance classes not only improve physical fitness but also promote creativity and self-expression. Physical education programs in schools play a crucial role in ensuring that all children have access to regular exercise and learn the importance of maintaining an active lifestyle.

Unstructured play, on the other hand, allows children to explore their interests and engage in physical activity in a more spontaneous and self-directed manner. This type of play can take many forms, such as playing tag, riding a bike, climbing trees, or simply running around the playground. Unstructured play is essential for developing imagination and creativity, as it allows children to create their own games, set their own rules, and solve problems on their own. It also provides opportunities for children to practice social skills, such as negotiation, cooperation, and conflict resolution, as they interact with their peers.

Both structured exercise and unstructured play offer unique benefits and are essential for a balanced approach to physical activity. Encouraging children to participate in a variety of activities can help them develop a broad range of skills and interests while ensuring they remain engaged and motivated. It is important for parents and caregivers to provide opportunities for both types of physical activity and to create an environment that supports and encourages an active lifestyle.

One of the most significant benefits of regular physical activity is the improvement of physical health. Exercise helps children build strong muscles and bones, maintain a healthy weight, and improve cardiovascular fitness. Regular physical activity also reduces the risk of developing chronic health conditions, such as obesity, type 2 diabetes, and heart disease, later in life. For children, developing good exercise habits early on can set the foundation for a lifetime of healthy living. Additionally, physical activity can improve coordination, balance, and flexibility, which are essential for performing everyday tasks and participating in various sports and activities.

Exercise and play also have a profound impact on mental and emotional well-being. Physical activity stimulates the release of endorphins, which are chemicals in the brain that promote feelings of happiness and reduce stress. Regular exercise can help alleviate symptoms of anxiety and depression, improve mood, and boost overall mental health. For children, engaging in physical activity can provide an outlet for energy and emotions, helping them manage stress and cope with the challenges of daily life. Furthermore, active play can enhance self-esteem and confidence, as children achieve new milestones and master new skills.

Cognitive development is another critical area influenced by exercise and play. Physical activity has been shown to improve concentration, memory, and academic performance. When children engage in active play, they are often required to think critically, solve problems, and make decisions, all of which contribute to cognitive growth. Additionally, physical activity increases blood flow to the brain, providing it with the oxygen and nutrients it needs to function optimally. Incorporating regular exercise into a child's routine can therefore enhance their ability to learn and succeed in school.

Social skills are also developed and strengthened through exercise and play. When children participate in group activities, they learn how to communicate effectively, work as part of a team, and resolve conflicts. These interactions teach valuable lessons about empathy, cooperation, and respect for others. For example, playing team sports requires children to work together towards a common goal, understand their roles within the team, and support their teammates. These experiences help children build strong relationships and develop the social competencies needed to navigate various social situations throughout their lives.

Promoting physical activity in children requires a concerted effort from parents, caregivers, schools, and communities. One of the most effective ways to encourage children to be active is to model an active lifestyle. When children see their parents and caregivers engaging in regular physical activity and enjoying it, they are more likely to adopt similar habits. Families can make physical activity a regular part of their routine by participating in activities together, such as going for walks, riding bikes, or playing sports. Creating a culture of activity within the family can instill a love for exercise and play that lasts a lifetime.

Providing a safe and supportive environment for physical activity is also crucial. Access to safe playgrounds, parks, and recreational facilities can encourage children to be active and explore different forms of exercise and play. Schools play a vital role in promoting physical activity by offering quality physical education programs and opportunities for students to participate in sports and other extracurricular activities. Communities can support active lifestyles by organizing events, such as fun runs, sports leagues, and fitness classes, that encourage children and families to get moving.

Limiting screen time and sedentary behaviors is another important aspect of promoting physical activity. With the increasing prevalence of electronic devices and screen-based entertainment, it is essential to set boundaries and encourage children to spend more time being active. Establishing screen-free times, such as during meals and before bedtime, and encouraging outdoor play can help reduce sedentary behavior and increase physical activity levels. Providing alternatives to screen time, such as books, puzzles, and creative toys, can also keep children engaged and active.

Incorporating physical activity into daily routines can make it easier for children to meet the recommended levels of exercise. Simple changes, such as walking or biking to school, taking the stairs instead of the elevator, and incorporating active breaks during homework or study time, can add up to significant amounts of physical activity over the course of a day. Encouraging children to participate in household chores, such as gardening, cleaning, or washing the car, can also provide opportunities for physical activity while teaching responsibility and life skills.

It is important to recognize and celebrate the diverse interests and abilities of children when promoting physical activity. Every child is unique, and what motivates one child to be active may not work for another. Offering a variety of activities and allowing children to choose the ones they enjoy most can help ensure they remain engaged and enthusiastic about exercise and play. Whether it is organized sports, dance, martial arts, swimming, or simply playing in the backyard, finding activities that resonate with a child's interests can foster a lifelong love of physical activity.

Addressing barriers to physical activity is also essential for promoting active lifestyles. Factors such as lack of time, access to facilities, safety concerns, and financial constraints can all impact a child's ability to engage in regular exercise and play. Identifying and addressing these barriers requires collaboration between parents, schools, and communities. For example, schools can provide after-school programs that offer supervised physical activities, while communities can invest in safe and accessible recreational spaces. Parents can advocate for policies and programs that support physical activity and work to create a home environment that prioritizes active living.

In addition to promoting physical health, exercise and play can also foster a sense of joy and fulfillment in children. Physical activity should be fun and enjoyable, not just a task to be completed. Encouraging children to explore different activities and find what they love can help them develop a positive attitude towards exercise and play. Celebrating achievements, whether big or small, and providing positive reinforcement can motivate children to stay active and continue pursuing their interests.

Ultimately, the goal is to create a balanced and active lifestyle that supports the overall well-being of children. By promoting regular physical activity through exercise and play, parents and caregivers can help children develop the physical, mental, and emotional skills needed to lead healthy and fulfilling lives. The benefits of an active lifestyle extend far beyond childhood, laying the foundation for a lifetime of good health and happiness. Through a combination of structured exercise, unstructured play, and supportive environments, we can nurture a generation of children who are strong, resilient, and ready to take on the world

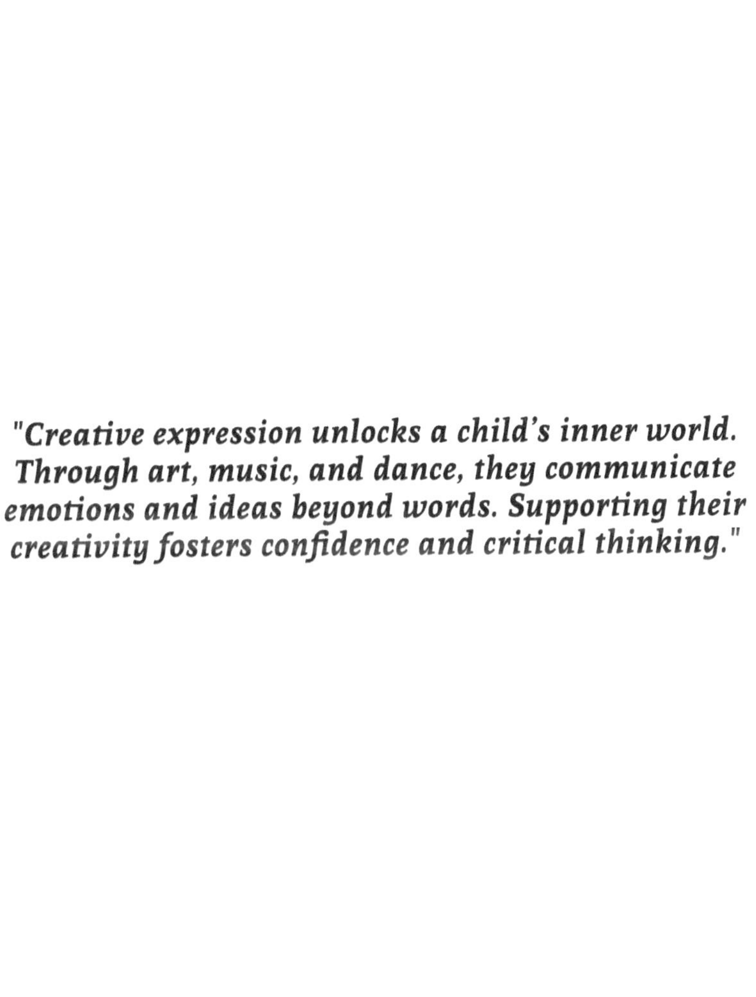

"Creative expression unlocks a child's inner world. Through art, music, and dance, they communicate emotions and ideas beyond words. Supporting their creativity fosters confidence and critical thinking."

SEVEN

Mindfulness Moments: Teaching Calm and Focus

Mindfulness is a transformative practice that can significantly enhance children's ability to remain calm, focused, and emotionally resilient. Teaching mindfulness moments involves incorporating simple yet effective techniques into daily routines, helping children develop a heightened awareness of the present moment and a deeper sense of inner peace. Mindfulness is not solely about meditation; it encompasses a variety of practices designed to help children understand and manage their emotions, reduce stress, and improve concentration. By integrating mindfulness into their lives, children can establish a foundation of mental well-being that supports their overall growth and development.

One of the most accessible ways to introduce mindfulness to children is through deep breathing exercises. Teaching children to pay attention to their breath can have an immediate calming effect, helping to soothe the mind and body. Simple techniques like belly breathing, where children place their hands on their stomachs and feel it rise and fall with each breath, can be very effective. Another method is to count breaths, such as inhaling for a count of four, holding for four, and then exhaling for four. These exercises can be practiced anywhere and anytime, making them a versatile tool for managing stress and enhancing focus.

The body scan is another mindfulness technique that can help children connect with their bodies and become more aware of physical sensations. This practice involves guiding children to focus on different parts of their body, starting from the toes and moving up to the head, noticing any sensations without judgment. This exercise helps children develop a deeper awareness of their physical state, which can be particularly useful for relaxation and grounding. The body scan can be done while lying down, sitting, or even standing, making it adaptable to various settings and needs.

Mindful listening is an engaging practice that can help children enhance their focus and presence. This involves listening to sounds with full attention, whether it is the sound of nature, music, or even a bell or chime. Children can close their eyes and focus on the sounds around them, noticing the different qualities of each sound. This practice not only helps children develop concentration but also encourages them to appreciate the richness of their auditory environment and develop a greater sense of awareness.

Incorporating mindfulness into daily activities can make the practice more natural and sustainable. For example, children can be taught to eat mindfully by paying full attention to the experience of eating. This involves noticing the colors, textures, and tastes of the food, chewing slowly, and savoring each bite. Mindful eating enhances the sensory experience of food, promotes healthier eating habits, and fosters a greater appreciation for nourishment. Parents can model this behavior and create a mindful eating environment by eliminating distractions such as television or electronic devices during meals.

Mindful movement is another way to integrate mindfulness into a child's routine. Activities such as yoga, tai chi, or simple stretching exercises help children connect with their bodies and develop a sense of calm and focus. These activities combine physical movement with mindful awareness, encouraging children to pay attention to their body's sensations and movements. Yoga, in particular, has been shown to improve flexibility, strength, and balance while also promoting relaxation and stress reduction. Incorporating mindful movement into a child's day can be a fun and engaging way to practice mindfulness while also supporting physical health.

Gratitude practices can also be a powerful component of mindfulness for children. Encouraging children to reflect on and express gratitude for the positive aspects of their lives can help shift their focus from negative thoughts to positive ones. This can be done through simple practices such as keeping a gratitude journal, where children write down things they are thankful for each day, or sharing gratitude at the dinner table. Practicing gratitude helps children develop a positive mindset and fosters a sense of appreciation for the world around them.

Visualization is another mindfulness technique that can help children develop calm and focus. Guided imagery exercises involve using the imagination to create calming and positive mental images. Children can be guided to visualize a peaceful place, such as a beach or a forest, and imagine themselves in that setting, noticing the sights, sounds, and sensations. This practice helps children relax and reduce anxiety, providing a mental escape from stressors. Visualization can be particularly useful before bedtime, helping children transition to sleep with a sense of calm and security.

Teaching children to recognize and label their emotions is a fundamental aspect of mindfulness. By helping children identify what they are feeling and understand that emotions are temporary and manageable, parents and caregivers can support emotional regulation and resilience. Simple practices such as the "feelings wheel" or emotion cards can help children learn to articulate their emotions and develop a vocabulary for discussing their inner experiences. Encouraging open and non-judgmental conversations about emotions can create a supportive environment where children feel safe to express themselves and seek help when needed.

Mindfulness can also be practiced through creative activities such as drawing, painting, or crafting. These activities allow children to express themselves and focus on the present moment, engaging their senses and creativity. Encouraging children to approach these activities mindfully, paying attention to the colors, textures, and movements involved, can enhance the calming and centering effects. Creative mindfulness activities provide an outlet for self-expression and can be a therapeutic way for children to process their thoughts and emotions.

Incorporating nature into mindfulness practice can deepen the experience and provide additional benefits. Spending time outdoors and connecting with nature is inherently calming and grounding. Activities such as nature walks, gardening, or simply observing the natural environment help children develop a sense of wonder and appreciation for the world around them. Mindful nature activities encourage children to fully engage their senses, noticing the sights, sounds, and smells of the natural world. This connection with nature fosters a sense of peace and well-being while also promoting physical activity and outdoor exploration.

Parents and caregivers play a crucial role in supporting and modeling mindfulness for children. Demonstrating mindfulness in everyday life, such as taking moments to breathe deeply, practicing gratitude, or approaching tasks with full attention, sets a positive example for children to follow. Creating a family culture that values mindfulness and integrates it into daily routines can help children develop consistent mindfulness practices. Openly discussing the benefits of mindfulness and encouraging children to share their experiences can further reinforce the importance of these practices.

Schools and educational institutions can also play a significant role in promoting mindfulness. Integrating mindfulness practices into the classroom, such as starting the day with a few minutes of deep breathing or incorporating mindfulness breaks during lessons, can support students' focus and emotional regulation. Teachers can receive training in mindfulness techniques and incorporate them into their teaching strategies, creating a supportive and calm learning environment. School-wide initiatives, such as mindfulness programs or workshops, can further promote the adoption of mindfulness practices among students and staff.

Mindfulness apps and resources can also be valuable tools for teaching mindfulness to children. There are numerous apps designed specifically for children that offer guided meditations, breathing exercises, and mindfulness activities. These resources provide structured and engaging ways for children to practice mindfulness and can be easily integrated into daily routines. Parents can explore these options and find the ones that best suit their child's needs and preferences.

It is important to recognize that mindfulness is a skill that develops over time and requires regular practice. Encouraging children to be patient with themselves and approach mindfulness with a sense of curiosity and openness can help them stay motivated and engaged. Consistency is key, and even short, daily mindfulness practices can have a significant impact on a child's well-being. Celebrating progress and acknowledging the benefits of mindfulness can reinforce the value of these practices and encourage children to continue incorporating them into their lives.

In conclusion, teaching mindfulness moments to children is a valuable investment in their mental, emotional, and physical well-being. By integrating simple mindfulness practices into daily routines, parents and caregivers can help children develop calmness, focus, and resilience. Mindfulness techniques such as deep breathing, body scans, mindful listening, mindful eating, and mindful movement can be easily adapted to suit different settings and needs. Creative activities, gratitude practices, visualization, and nature experiences further enrich the mindfulness journey. Through consistent practice, modeling, and support, children can cultivate a foundation of mindfulness that enhances their overall quality of life and prepares them to navigate the challenges and opportunities of the world with greater awareness and balance.

"Goal setting inspires ambition and achievement. Breaking down goals into manageable steps makes them attainable. Celebrating progress along the way motivates continued effort and success."

EIGHT

READING TOGETHER: CULTIVATING A LOVE FOR BOOKS

Reading together is one of the most enriching and impactful activities parents and caregivers can engage in with children. It fosters a love for books, enhances literacy skills, and strengthens the bond between adult and child. Cultivating a love for books from an early age sets the foundation for lifelong learning and curiosity. The benefits of reading together extend beyond academic achievement, promoting emotional development, empathy, and imagination. To nurture a deep and lasting love for books, it is essential to create a positive and engaging reading environment, select appropriate and captivating books, and integrate reading into daily routines.

The journey to fostering a love for books begins with creating a welcoming and stimulating reading environment. A cozy reading nook with comfortable seating, good lighting, and a variety of books within easy reach can make reading a pleasurable and anticipated activity. Allowing children to have a say in decorating their reading space can also make it more inviting and personal. Keeping books accessible encourages spontaneous reading and allows children to explore books at their own pace. Rotating the selection of books to include a mix of favorites and new titles can keep the reading material fresh and exciting.

Choosing the right books is crucial for engaging children and nurturing their love for reading. It is important to consider the child's age, interests, and reading level when selecting books. For young children, picture books with vibrant illustrations and simple, rhythmic text can capture their attention and imagination. As children grow, introducing a variety of genres, such as fairy tales, adventure stories, mysteries, and non-fiction, can help them discover their preferences and expand their horizons. Including books that reflect the child's experiences, culture, and identity can also enhance their connection to the stories and characters.

Reading together is not just about the words on the page; it is about the shared experience and the interactions that occur during reading. Making reading a collaborative and interactive activity can deepen the child's engagement and enjoyment. Asking open-ended questions about the story, discussing the characters' actions and emotions, and encouraging the child to predict what will happen next can make reading an active and thought-provoking experience. This dialogue not only enhances comprehension but also helps children develop critical thinking and verbal skills.

Storytelling is an art, and how a story is read can significantly impact a child's enjoyment and understanding. Using expressive voices for different characters, varying the tone and pace of reading, and incorporating gestures and facial expressions can bring the story to life. Children are more likely to be captivated by a lively and animated reading than a monotone delivery. Encouraging children to participate in the storytelling, such as by reading aloud parts of the text or acting out scenes, can also make the experience more dynamic and fun.

Establishing a regular reading routine can help integrate reading into a child's daily life and make it a consistent and valued activity. Designating specific times for reading, such as before bedtime or after school, can create a sense of ritual and anticipation. Reading before bedtime, in particular, can be a calming and bonding activity that helps children wind down and transition to sleep. Consistency in the reading routine helps children associate reading with relaxation and enjoyment, reinforcing their love for books.

Beyond the home, there are many opportunities to cultivate a love for books. Visiting libraries and bookstores can be exciting outings that expose children to a wide range of books and foster a sense of community. Participating in storytime sessions, book clubs, or author events can enhance the reading experience and allow children to share their love for books with others. Libraries often offer programs and activities that encourage reading, such as summer reading challenges or themed storytimes, which can motivate children to read more and discover new interests.

Encouraging children to see themselves as readers and authors can also deepen their connection to books. Providing opportunities for children to create their own stories, whether through drawing, writing, or dictating to an adult, can empower them and enhance their appreciation for storytelling. Displaying children's books and writing in a special place, such as a bulletin board or bookshelf, can give them a sense of pride and accomplishment. Celebrating their creations and sharing them with family and friends reinforces the value of their contributions and encourages a love for literature.

Digital media can also play a role in fostering a love for books, especially in an increasingly digital world. E-books, audiobooks, and interactive reading apps can complement traditional reading and provide additional ways for children to engage with stories. Audiobooks, in particular, can be a great way to enjoy books during car rides or quiet time, and they can also be helpful for children who struggle with reading independently. However, it is important to balance digital and traditional reading to ensure that screen time does not overshadow the tactile and immersive experience of reading a physical book.

Creating a positive and supportive reading environment also involves being mindful of the challenges and barriers that some children may face. Children with learning disabilities, such as dyslexia, may require additional support and resources to develop their reading skills. It is important to provide patience, encouragement, and appropriate accommodations, such as audiobooks, large-print books, or specialized reading programs, to help these children succeed. Collaborating with teachers, reading specialists, and other professionals can also ensure that children receive the support they need to thrive as readers.

Modeling a love for reading is one of the most effective ways to inspire children to become avid readers. When children see their parents and caregivers enjoying books and prioritizing reading, they are more likely to adopt similar habits. Sharing personal experiences with books, discussing favorite stories, and making time for family reading sessions can demonstrate the joy and value of reading. Creating a family culture that celebrates and values books can have a lasting impact on children's attitudes towards reading.

Reading together also provides an opportunity to address and discuss important topics and values. Books can be a window into different cultures, perspectives, and experiences, fostering empathy and understanding. Reading stories that address themes such as kindness, bravery, friendship, and perseverance can provide valuable lessons and promote positive character development.

Discussions about the messages and morals of stories can help children apply these lessons to their own lives and develop a deeper understanding of the world around them.

The benefits of reading together extend beyond childhood and can have a lasting impact on a person's life. Children who develop a love for books are more likely to continue reading into adulthood, reaping the cognitive, emotional, and social benefits that reading provides. Lifelong readers often experience improved mental health, increased empathy, and greater cultural awareness. By fostering a love for books from an early age, parents and caregivers can contribute to a child's lifelong journey of learning and personal growth.

In summary, reading together is a powerful and enriching activity that can cultivate a love for books and support a child's overall development. Creating a welcoming reading environment, selecting engaging and appropriate books, and making reading a regular and interactive part of daily life can foster a deep and lasting appreciation for literature. Encouraging creative expression, participating in community reading activities, and modeling a love for reading can further enhance the reading experience and inspire children to become lifelong readers. Through the shared joy of reading, parents and caregivers can strengthen their bond with children and open doors to a world of imagination, knowledge, and empathy.

ᐅᐅᐅ

"Time management is a crucial life skill. Teaching children to prioritize tasks helps them balance responsibilities and leisure. This discipline enhances productivity and overall well-being."

NINE
SCREEN TIME BALANCE: MANAGING DIGITAL CONSUMPTION

Screen time balance is a crucial aspect of modern parenting, as digital consumption has become an integral part of children's lives. With the rise of smartphones, tablets, computers, and televisions, children are exposed to screens more than ever before. While technology can offer educational benefits and entertainment, excessive screen time can have detrimental effects on physical health, mental well-being, and social development. Therefore, it is essential for parents and caregivers to manage digital consumption effectively, promoting a healthy balance between screen time and other activities.

The first step in managing screen time is understanding its potential impact on children. Excessive screen time has been linked to various health issues, such as obesity, sleep problems, and vision strain. Physical inactivity due to prolonged screen use can lead to weight gain and related health problems. Additionally, exposure to blue light from screens, especially before bedtime, can disrupt sleep patterns by interfering with the production of melatonin, the hormone that regulates sleep. Children who spend a lot of time on screens are also at risk of developing digital eye strain, which can cause discomfort and affect vision.

Mental health is another area affected by excessive screen time. Studies have shown that high levels of screen use can contribute to anxiety, depression, and decreased emotional well-being. Social media, in particular, can expose children to unrealistic standards, cyberbullying, and peer pressure, negatively impacting their self-esteem and mental health. Moreover, excessive screen time can reduce opportunities for face-to-face interactions, which are crucial for developing social skills and emotional intelligence.

To mitigate these risks, it is important to establish clear and consistent screen time guidelines. The American Academy of Pediatrics (AAP) recommends that children aged 2 to 5 years should have no more than one hour of screen time per day, and for children aged 6 and older, parents should set consistent limits on the amount of time spent on screens, ensuring it does not interfere with sleep, physical activity, or other essential behaviors. Creating a family media plan can help establish these guidelines and ensure that all family members are on the same page regarding digital consumption.

Setting boundaries around screen use involves creating specific rules and schedules. For instance, parents can designate certain times of the day as screen-free, such as during meals, family time, or the hour before bedtime. Establishing screen-free zones, such as bedrooms and dining areas, can also help reduce screen time and promote healthier habits. Encouraging children to take regular breaks during screen use, such as the 20-20-20 rule (taking a 20-second break every 20 minutes to look at something 20 feet away), can help reduce eye strain and encourage physical movement.

Modeling healthy screen habits is crucial, as children often imitate the behavior of their parents and caregivers. By demonstrating balanced screen use, such as limiting personal screen time, engaging in offline activities, and prioritizing face-to-face interactions, parents can set a positive example for their children. Additionally, discussing the reasons behind screen time limits and the benefits of a balanced lifestyle can help children understand the importance of managing their digital consumption.

Encouraging alternative activities is another effective strategy for managing screen time. Providing opportunities for physical activity, such as outdoor play, sports, or family walks, can help children develop a love for movement and reduce their reliance on screens for entertainment. Creative activities, such as drawing, reading, or playing musical instruments, can stimulate imagination and cognitive development. Social activities, such as playdates, family game nights, or community events, can foster social skills and strengthen relationships.

Incorporating educational content into screen time can also be beneficial. Educational apps, games, and programs can support learning and development when used appropriately. Parents can select high-quality, age-appropriate content that aligns with their child's interests and educational goals. Co-viewing and engaging with children during screen time can enhance the learning experience and provide opportunities for discussion and interaction.

Monitoring and managing online content is essential for ensuring a safe digital environment. Parents should be aware of the websites, apps, and social media platforms their children use and ensure that privacy settings are enabled. Utilizing parental control tools and software can help restrict access to inappropriate content and monitor online activity. It is important to have open and ongoing conversations with children about online safety, including topics such as cyberbullying, privacy, and responsible online behavior.

Balancing screen time also involves addressing the potential for technology addiction. Some children may develop an unhealthy attachment to screens, leading to compulsive use and difficulty disengaging from digital devices. Recognizing the signs of technology addiction, such as increased irritability when screen time is limited, neglecting responsibilities, or losing interest in offline activities, is crucial for early intervention. Establishing firm boundaries, providing alternative activities, and seeking professional help if necessary can help address and prevent technology addiction.

Promoting a healthy digital diet requires a holistic approach that considers the quality and quantity of screen time. It is important to distinguish between passive screen time, such as watching videos, and active screen time, such as engaging in educational games or creating digital content. Encouraging a balance between different types of screen activities can enhance the overall benefits of digital consumption while minimizing its negative effects. Parents can also emphasize the importance of digital detox, encouraging periodic breaks from screens to reconnect with the physical world and recharge.

Technology can also be harnessed to promote physical activity and healthy habits. Fitness apps, virtual workout classes, and interactive games that require physical movement can motivate children to stay active while using screens. Parents can participate in these activities with their children, making exercise a fun and shared experience. Additionally, using technology to set reminders for breaks, hydration, and outdoor time can help children develop a balanced routine that incorporates healthy habits.

Schools and educational institutions play a significant role in managing screen time and promoting digital literacy. Incorporating screen time guidelines into school policies, providing education on responsible digital use, and encouraging physical activity and offline learning can help create a balanced approach to technology in education. Collaboration between parents, teachers, and administrators is essential for reinforcing consistent messages about screen time management and ensuring a supportive environment for students.

Community programs and initiatives can also support families in managing screen time. Local organizations, libraries, and recreational centers can offer activities and resources that encourage offline engagement and social interaction. Community events, such as outdoor movie nights, sports leagues, and family workshops, provide opportunities for families to connect and participate in screen-free activities. By fostering a community culture that values balanced digital consumption, families can find support and motivation to maintain healthy screen habits.

Addressing the challenges of screen time balance requires ongoing effort and adaptability. As technology continues to evolve, parents and caregivers must stay informed about new trends and potential risks associated with digital consumption. Regularly reassessing screen time guidelines, discussing digital experiences with children, and seeking feedback on what works and what doesn't can help refine strategies and ensure they remain effective. Flexibility and a willingness to adjust approaches as children grow and their needs change are essential for maintaining a balanced digital lifestyle.

Ultimately, the goal is to create a harmonious relationship with technology that enhances rather than detracts from overall well-being. By managing screen time effectively, parents and caregivers can help children develop a healthy balance between digital consumption and other important aspects of life, such as physical activity, social interaction, and creative pursuits. This balanced approach not only supports physical health but also fosters mental and emotional resilience, preparing children to navigate the digital world with confidence and responsibility.

Promoting screen time balance is not about eliminating technology from children's lives but about integrating it thoughtfully and purposefully. By prioritizing quality content, setting clear boundaries, and encouraging diverse activities, parents can help children reap the benefits of technology while minimizing its potential drawbacks. Open communication, consistent modeling of healthy habits, and a supportive environment are key to achieving this balance and ensuring that children grow up with a positive and well-rounded relationship with digital media.

In conclusion, managing digital consumption and achieving screen time balance is a multifaceted task that requires careful consideration and proactive effort from parents, caregivers, and the wider community. By understanding the potential impacts of excessive screen time and implementing practical strategies to promote a balanced lifestyle, we can support the healthy development of children in a digital age. Encouraging physical activity, fostering creativity, enhancing social skills, and prioritizing mental well-being are all integral parts of this process. With thoughtful guidance and support, children can learn to navigate the digital landscape in a way that enriches their lives and contributes to their overall health and happiness.

ᗡᗡᗡ

"Positive self-talk is a powerful tool for building confidence. Guiding children to replace negative thoughts with affirming ones strengthens their self-esteem. This practice helps them face challenges with resilience."

TEN

KINDNESS COUNTS: ENCOURAGING EMPATHY AND COMPASSION

Kindness is a fundamental human quality that contributes to personal happiness and the well-being of society. Encouraging empathy and compassion in children is essential for fostering a more harmonious and understanding world. Teaching kindness involves helping children recognize and respond to the feelings and needs of others, promoting acts of generosity, and creating a culture of respect and empathy. Through intentional practices and modeling, parents, educators, and caregivers can cultivate these values in children, guiding them to develop into compassionate and empathetic individuals.

One of the most effective ways to encourage kindness is by modeling empathetic behavior. Children learn by observing the actions and attitudes of the adults around them. When parents and caregivers consistently demonstrate kindness, empathy, and compassion in their interactions with others, children are more likely to adopt these behaviors. Simple acts, such as offering help to a neighbor, expressing gratitude, or showing patience and understanding, can have a profound impact on a child's perception of kindness. Discussing these actions and explaining why they are important can further reinforce the value of empathy and compassion.

Creating opportunities for children to practice kindness is crucial for developing these qualities. Encouraging children to perform small acts of kindness, such as sharing their toys, helping a friend, or writing thank-you notes, helps them understand the positive impact of their actions. These experiences teach children that kindness can be simple yet powerful, fostering a sense of satisfaction and connection. Parents and educators can set up activities or challenges that focus on performing kind deeds, making kindness a fun and engaging practice.

Empathy, the ability to understand and share the feelings of others, is a key component of kindness. Teaching children to recognize and name their own emotions is the first step in developing empathy. When children can identify what they are feeling, they are better equipped to understand the emotions of others. Encouraging open discussions about feelings and validating children's emotions can help them become more attuned to their own and others' emotional states. Storytelling and reading books that explore different emotions and perspectives can also enhance empathy by allowing children to step into the shoes of various characters and understand their experiences.

Role-playing and perspective-taking activities are effective tools for teaching empathy. These activities involve encouraging children to imagine how others might feel in different situations and to consider the perspectives of those who may have different experiences or backgrounds. For example, children can role-play scenarios where they practice comforting a friend who is upset or standing up for someone who is being treated unfairly. These exercises help children develop the ability to see the world from different viewpoints, fostering a deeper understanding of and compassion for others.

Acts of service and community involvement are powerful ways to teach kindness and empathy. Participating in community service projects, such as volunteering at a local food bank, helping clean up a park, or visiting a nursing home, allows children to see the tangible effects of their kindness and understand the importance of contributing to their community. These experiences can be both humbling and empowering, showing children that even small actions can make a significant difference in the lives of others. Parents and educators can facilitate these opportunities and encourage children to reflect on their experiences and the impact of their contributions.

Creating a culture of kindness within the home or classroom is essential for reinforcing these values. Establishing norms and expectations that prioritize respect, empathy, and cooperation helps children internalize these principles. This can include setting guidelines for positive behavior, such as using kind words, listening actively, and resolving conflicts peacefully. Recognizing and celebrating acts of kindness, whether through verbal praise, rewards, or a kindness chart, reinforces the importance of these behaviors and motivates children to continue practicing them.

Mindfulness practices can also support the development of empathy and compassion. Mindfulness involves paying attention to the present moment with an open and non-judgmental attitude. Teaching children mindfulness techniques, such as deep breathing, meditation, and body scans, can help them become more aware of their own emotions and more sensitive to the feelings of others. Compassion meditation, a specific type of mindfulness practice, focuses on cultivating feelings of compassion and kindness towards oneself and others. This practice involves visualizing sending positive thoughts and wishes to others, fostering a sense of connection and empathy.

Encouraging reflective practices can deepen children's understanding of kindness and empathy. Journaling or discussing experiences of kindness, both giving and receiving, allows children to process their emotions and thoughts. Reflecting on questions such as "How did it feel to help someone?" or "What did you learn from being kind?" can help children internalize the value of empathy and understand its impact. These reflections can also highlight the interconnectedness of people and the importance of considering others' well-being.

The language used in conversations with children can significantly influence their understanding of empathy and kindness. Using inclusive and respectful language, avoiding negative labels, and emphasizing the positive qualities in others helps create a supportive environment. When discussing conflicts or negative behaviors, focusing on the impact of actions on others and encouraging problem-solving and restitution fosters a more empathetic approach. This perspective encourages children to consider the consequences of their actions and to think about how they can make amends and improve relationships.

The arts can also play a role in fostering empathy and compassion. Engaging in activities such as drawing, painting, music, and drama provides children with creative outlets for expressing their emotions and exploring different perspectives. Artistic activities can facilitate discussions about feelings and experiences, helping children develop a deeper understanding of themselves and others. Collaborative projects, such as group art installations or performances, encourage cooperation, communication, and shared empathy, reinforcing the value of working together towards a common goal.

Promoting diversity and inclusion is integral to teaching kindness and empathy. Exposing children to different cultures, traditions, and perspectives helps them appreciate the richness of human diversity and understand the experiences of others. Encouraging friendships and interactions with peers from various backgrounds fosters a sense of belonging and mutual respect. Addressing stereotypes and prejudices and promoting inclusive attitudes help children develop a more compassionate and open-minded view of the world. Celebrating cultural events, reading diverse books, and discussing global issues can broaden children's horizons and deepen their empathy.

Digital citizenship education is increasingly important in today's connected world. Teaching children about responsible and respectful online behavior helps them navigate the digital landscape with empathy and kindness. This includes understanding the impact of cyberbullying, practicing respectful communication, and being mindful of the information they share and consume. Encouraging children to use technology to support positive causes, such as participating in online campaigns for social justice or creating content that promotes kindness, empowers them to make a positive difference in the digital world.

Developing kindness and empathy also involves addressing and managing conflict in constructive ways. Teaching children conflict resolution skills, such as active listening, expressing feelings assertively, and finding mutually agreeable solutions, helps them handle disagreements with empathy and respect. Role-playing conflict scenarios and discussing the importance of understanding different perspectives can prepare children to navigate conflicts more effectively. Encouraging children to seek help from trusted adults when needed and to practice forgiveness and reconciliation reinforces the importance of maintaining positive relationships.

Family and school environments that support open communication and emotional safety provide a strong foundation for teaching kindness and empathy. When children feel heard, valued, and understood, they are more likely to extend these attitudes towards others. Creating spaces where children can share their thoughts and feelings without fear of judgment or criticism fosters a sense of trust and belonging. This supportive environment encourages children to express kindness and empathy freely and to seek support when they need it.

In summary, teaching kindness and encouraging empathy and compassion in children is a multifaceted process that involves modeling empathetic behavior, creating opportunities for kindness, and fostering a supportive environment. Through intentional practices, such as role-playing, community service, mindfulness, and reflection, children can develop a deeper understanding of and commitment to these values. By promoting diversity, inclusion, and responsible digital citizenship, parents, educators, and caregivers can guide children in becoming compassionate and empathetic individuals who contribute positively to their communities and the world. The cultivation of kindness and empathy not only enhances personal well-being but also builds a more connected, understanding, and harmonious society.

ᗡᗡᗡ

"Problem-solving skills equip children to navigate life's complexities. Encouraging a systematic approach to challenges fosters critical thinking. This ability to find solutions builds independence and adaptability."

ELEVEN

Chore Time: Teaching Responsibility and Cooperation

Teaching children responsibility and cooperation through chores is a vital part of their development. Chores provide practical lessons in responsibility, teamwork, and the value of contributing to the family and community. When children are involved in household tasks, they learn essential life skills that build character and foster a sense of accomplishment and self-worth. Integrating chores into a child's routine can be approached in a way that is engaging, educational, and supportive, creating a positive experience that benefits both the child and the family.

Introducing chores to children at a young age sets the foundation for a lifetime of responsibility. Even toddlers can participate in simple tasks like picking up toys or helping to set the table. These early experiences help children understand that they are part of a family unit where everyone contributes.

It is important to choose age-appropriate tasks that match the child's abilities, ensuring that chores are achievable and not overwhelming. Gradually increasing the complexity of tasks as the child grows builds confidence and competence.

One of the key benefits of assigning chores is that it teaches children about responsibility. When children are given tasks to complete, they learn to take ownership of their duties. This sense of responsibility is reinforced when they understand that their efforts contribute to the well-being of the family. Completing chores on time and to a certain standard helps children develop a sense of accountability and pride in their work. It also teaches them to manage their time effectively and prioritize tasks.

Chores also provide an excellent opportunity to teach cooperation and teamwork. Many household tasks require collaboration, and when children work together with family members, they learn the value of cooperation. Tasks such as cooking, cleaning, or gardening can become team activities where everyone has a role to play.

This collaborative effort fosters communication, problem-solving, and mutual support. Children learn to appreciate the contributions of others and understand that working together makes tasks easier and more enjoyable.

To make chore time more engaging, parents can introduce creative and fun elements. Turning chores into games or challenges can motivate children and make the tasks feel less like work. For example, setting a timer and challenging children to complete a task before it goes off can add an element of excitement. Playing upbeat music during chore time can also make the experience more enjoyable. Reward systems, such as sticker charts or earning points for completed tasks, can provide additional motivation and a sense of achievement.

It is important to communicate clearly about expectations and instructions for chores. Providing detailed explanations and demonstrations can help children understand how to complete tasks correctly. Using visual aids, such as chore charts or checklists, can also be helpful.

These tools provide a clear and consistent reminder of what needs to be done and can help children track their progress. Encouraging children to ask questions and seek clarification fosters a learning environment where they feel supported and confident in their abilities.

Positive reinforcement and praise are crucial for reinforcing good habits and motivating children to continue their efforts. Acknowledging and celebrating their accomplishments, no matter how small, boosts their self-esteem and reinforces the value of their contributions. Specific praise that highlights the effort and the positive impact of their work is particularly effective.

For example, saying "You did a great job cleaning your room. It looks so neat and organized!" helps children see the tangible results of their efforts and encourages them to maintain these habits.

In addition to teaching responsibility and cooperation, chores help children develop a range of practical skills that are essential for independent living. Tasks such as cooking, cleaning, laundry, and basic home maintenance equip children with the knowledge and abilities they will need as adults.

These skills contribute to their self-sufficiency and confidence in managing their own households in the future. By involving children in a variety of tasks, parents can ensure they gain a comprehensive set of skills.

Chores also provide valuable lessons in organization and time management. When children have regular chores, they learn to integrate these tasks into their daily routines. This requires them to plan their time effectively and balance their responsibilities with other activities, such as homework and leisure. Developing these organizational skills helps children become more efficient and disciplined, qualities that are beneficial in all areas of life.

Involving children in household chores can also strengthen family bonds. Working together on common tasks provides opportunities for meaningful interactions and shared experiences.

These moments can lead to conversations, laughter, and a sense of camaraderie. Children feel a greater sense of belonging and connection when they actively participate in family activities. This collaborative environment fosters a sense of unity and mutual support within the family.

To ensure that chore time remains a positive and productive experience, it is important to approach it with flexibility and understanding. Each child is unique, and their interests, abilities, and levels of motivation may vary. Being attuned to these differences and adapting the approach accordingly can help maintain a positive attitude towards chores.

For example, allowing children to choose from a list of tasks or rotating chores to provide variety can keep them engaged and prevent boredom.

It is also important to address any resistance or reluctance towards chores with patience and empathy. Understanding the reasons behind a child's resistance, whether it is due to feeling overwhelmed, lack of interest, or simply not knowing how to do the task, can help parents provide appropriate support and encouragement. Creating a supportive environment where children feel heard and valued can reduce resistance and promote cooperation.

Teaching children about the broader impact of their contributions can also enhance their sense of responsibility and motivation. Helping children understand that their efforts benefit the entire family and contribute to a well-functioning household can give them a sense of purpose and pride. Discussing the importance of teamwork and mutual support in maintaining a happy and healthy home reinforces the value of their contributions.

Encouraging children to take initiative and show leadership in chore-related activities can further enhance their sense of responsibility and confidence. For example, assigning older children the role of "chore captain" for a day, where they oversee the completion of tasks and help younger siblings, can develop their leadership skills. Providing opportunities for children to suggest improvements or come up with their own systems for completing chores fosters creativity and a sense of ownership.

Parents and caregivers can also incorporate educational elements into chore time. For example, cooking can become a lesson in math and science as children measure ingredients and observe chemical reactions. Gardening can teach children about biology and the environment. These educational aspects make chores more enriching and engaging, turning them into valuable learning experiences.

Balancing chores with other responsibilities and activities is essential for maintaining a healthy and enjoyable routine. While it is important for children to contribute to household tasks, it is equally important to ensure they have time for play, relaxation, and pursuing their interests. Striking this balance helps prevent burnout and ensures that chores do not become a source of stress. Flexibility in scheduling and a balanced approach to responsibilities and leisure can help maintain a positive attitude towards chores.

In summary, teaching children responsibility and cooperation through chores is a multifaceted and rewarding endeavor. Chores provide practical lessons in accountability, teamwork, and the value of contributing to the family and community. By choosing age-appropriate tasks, making chore time engaging and fun, and providing clear instructions and positive reinforcement, parents can create a positive and supportive environment for children to develop these essential qualities. The skills and habits children acquire through chores will benefit them throughout their lives, fostering independence, confidence, and a sense of belonging. Through a thoughtful and flexible approach, parents can ensure that chore time is a valuable and enjoyable experience for the entire family.

ϷϷϷ

"Habit tracking celebrates incremental progress. Visualizing achievements through charts or journals reinforces positive behaviors. This consistent practice cultivates a sense of accomplishment and growth."

TWELVE

GOAL SETTING: INSPIRING AMBITION AND ACHIEVEMENT

Goal setting is a powerful tool for inspiring ambition and achievement in children. By teaching children how to set and pursue goals, parents and educators can help them develop essential skills such as planning, perseverance, and self-discipline. Setting and achieving goals fosters a sense of purpose and direction, encouraging children to strive for personal growth and success. It also builds confidence and resilience, as children learn to overcome obstacles and celebrate their accomplishments. Effective goal setting involves understanding the importance of goals, choosing appropriate and meaningful targets, creating actionable plans, and maintaining motivation and focus.

The first step in goal setting is helping children understand the value and purpose of setting goals. Goals provide a clear direction and help children focus their efforts on specific outcomes. They act as a roadmap, guiding children towards desired achievements and helping them prioritize their activities. By discussing the benefits of goal setting, such as increased motivation, a sense of accomplishment, and the development of important life skills, parents and educators can inspire children to embrace the practice.

Choosing the right goals is crucial for maintaining interest and motivation. Goals should be specific, measurable, achievable, relevant, and time-bound (SMART). Specific goals provide a clear and concrete target, making it easier for children to understand what they are working towards. Measurable goals allow children to track their progress and recognize when they have achieved their objectives. Achievable goals ensure that children set realistic and attainable targets, preventing frustration and discouragement. Relevant goals are meaningful and aligned with the child's interests and values, making them more engaging and motivating. Time-bound goals have a clear deadline, creating a sense of urgency and helping children stay focused.

To help children set appropriate goals, parents and educators can guide them through a brainstorming process. Encouraging children to think about their interests, strengths, and areas for improvement can help them identify meaningful and motivating goals. It is important to involve children in the goal-setting process, allowing them to take ownership of their targets and feel a sense of agency. By discussing different types of goals, such as academic, personal, or extracurricular, parents and educators can help children set a balanced and comprehensive set of objectives.

Once goals are established, creating an actionable plan is essential for turning aspirations into reality. Breaking down larger goals into smaller, manageable steps makes the process less overwhelming and more achievable. This approach, known as chunking, helps children focus on one task at a time and builds momentum as they complete each step. Creating a timeline with specific deadlines for each step can further enhance organization and time management skills. Visual aids, such as goal charts or checklists, can help children track their progress and stay motivated.

Maintaining motivation and focus throughout the goal-setting process is critical for success. Positive reinforcement and encouragement from parents and educators play a significant role in keeping children engaged and committed to their goals. Celebrating small victories and acknowledging progress helps build confidence and reinforces the value of perseverance. Providing constructive feedback and support during setbacks or challenges teaches children resilience and problem-solving skills. Encouraging a growth mindset, where children view challenges as opportunities for learning and growth, can help them stay motivated and maintain a positive attitude.

Goal setting is not only about achieving specific outcomes but also about developing important life skills. The process teaches children how to plan and organize their activities, manage their time effectively, and stay focused on their priorities. These skills are essential for academic success and personal growth. Goal setting also fosters self-discipline and perseverance, as children learn to stay committed to their targets despite obstacles and distractions. By experiencing the process of setting, working towards, and achieving goals, children develop a sense of self-efficacy and confidence in their abilities.

Reflecting on the goal-setting process and outcomes is an important aspect of learning and growth. Encouraging children to evaluate their progress, identify challenges, and recognize their achievements helps them understand what works and what doesn't. This reflection can guide future goal-setting efforts, helping children refine their strategies and approaches. Discussing what they have learned from the experience, both successes and setbacks, fosters a deeper understanding of the value of persistence and adaptability. This reflective practice also reinforces the importance of setting realistic and meaningful goals.

In addition to individual goals, collaborative goal setting can teach children the value of teamwork and cooperation. Group projects or family goals provide opportunities for children to work together towards a common objective. Collaborative goal setting fosters communication, problem-solving, and mutual support. It also helps children understand the importance of contributing to a group effort and the satisfaction of achieving shared success. By involving children in group goal-setting activities, parents and educators can teach them the principles of teamwork and collective achievement.

Role models and mentors can play a significant role in inspiring ambition and achievement through goal setting. Parents, teachers, and other influential adults can share their own experiences with setting and achieving goals, providing guidance and inspiration. Stories of perseverance and success from role models can motivate children to set their own goals and work towards them with determination. Mentors can also provide valuable feedback, encouragement, and support, helping children navigate challenges and stay focused on their objectives.

Creating a supportive and goal-oriented environment is essential for fostering ambition and achievement. Encouraging a culture of goal setting within the family, classroom, or community reinforces the importance of personal growth and continuous improvement. Providing resources and opportunities for children to pursue their goals, such as access to books, extracurricular activities, or learning materials, supports their efforts and aspirations. Celebrating achievements and milestones within the community creates a positive and motivating atmosphere, where children feel encouraged and valued.

Technology can also be a useful tool for goal setting and tracking. Various apps and online platforms offer goal-setting features, progress tracking, and reminders. These tools can help children stay organized and motivated, providing a visual representation of their progress and achievements. Parents and educators can explore different technological resources to find the ones that best support their children's goal-setting efforts.

Balancing goal setting with flexibility is important for maintaining a healthy and positive approach. While setting and pursuing goals is valuable, it is also essential to recognize the importance of rest, relaxation, and enjoyment. Encouraging children to take breaks, engage in leisure activities, and celebrate their achievements helps prevent burnout and maintains a balanced lifestyle. Flexibility in adjusting goals or timelines as needed teaches children to be adaptable and resilient, understanding that setbacks are a natural part of the process.

In summary, goal setting is a powerful and transformative practice that inspires ambition and achievement in children. By teaching children how to set and pursue meaningful goals, parents and educators can help them develop essential skills such as planning, perseverance, and self-discipline. Effective goal setting involves understanding the importance of goals, choosing appropriate and engaging targets, creating actionable plans, and maintaining motivation and focus. Through intentional guidance, positive reinforcement, and a supportive environment, children can cultivate a sense of purpose and direction, fostering personal growth and success. The skills and attitudes developed through goal setting will benefit children throughout their lives, empowering them to achieve their aspirations and contribute positively to their communities.

ϷϷϷ

"Mindfulness practices integrate seamlessly into daily routines. These moments of presence enhance emotional well-being and focus. Teaching mindfulness fosters a balanced and peaceful mindset."

THIRTEEN

Time Management: Developing Organizational Skills

Time management is an essential skill that lays the foundation for a productive and fulfilling life. Developing organizational skills in children helps them manage their time effectively, prioritize tasks, and achieve their goals. Teaching time management involves guiding children in understanding the value of time, setting realistic schedules, and using tools and techniques to stay organized. By fostering these skills early on, parents and educators can help children build habits that will benefit them throughout their lives, enabling them to navigate academic, personal, and future professional challenges with greater ease and efficiency.

Understanding the value of time is the first step in developing effective time management skills. Children need to recognize that time is a finite resource and that how they use it can significantly impact their productivity and well-being. This awareness can be fostered through discussions about the importance of balancing different activities, such as schoolwork, chores, hobbies, and rest. Parents and educators can illustrate how time spent on one activity affects the availability of time for others, helping children appreciate the need for thoughtful planning and prioritization.

Setting realistic schedules is a crucial aspect of time management. Children should learn to allocate their time in a way that reflects their priorities and responsibilities while also allowing for flexibility and relaxation. Creating a daily or weekly schedule can help children visualize their time commitments and ensure that they are dedicating sufficient time to each task. Parents and educators can guide children in breaking down larger tasks into smaller, manageable steps, assigning specific time slots for each step. This approach not only makes tasks less overwhelming but also provides a clear roadmap for completing them efficiently.

To create an effective schedule, children need to set realistic and achievable goals. Encouraging them to establish short-term and long-term goals helps them stay focused and motivated. Short-term goals, such as completing homework or practicing a musical instrument, provide immediate targets that can be accomplished within a day or week. Long-term goals, such as preparing for a major exam or completing a project, require sustained effort and planning over a more extended period. By balancing both types of goals, children can maintain a sense of progress and achievement while also working towards more significant objectives.

Using tools and techniques to stay organized is another key component of time management. Various tools, such as planners, calendars, and to-do lists, can help children keep track of their tasks and deadlines. Planners and calendars allow children to map out their schedules visually, providing a clear overview of their time commitments. To-do lists help children prioritize tasks and stay focused on what needs to be accomplished each day. Encouraging children to update these tools regularly and review their progress helps reinforce the habit of staying organized.

Technology can also play a valuable role in time management. There are numerous apps and digital tools designed to assist with scheduling, task management, and reminders. These tools can provide notifications and alerts to keep children on track with their responsibilities. Parents and educators can explore different options to find the ones that best suit their children's needs and preferences. However, it is essential to balance the use of technology with traditional methods to ensure that children develop a well-rounded approach to time management.

Teaching children to prioritize tasks is critical for effective time management. Not all tasks are of equal importance, and learning to differentiate between high-priority and low-priority activities helps children focus their efforts where they are most needed. One technique for prioritizing tasks is the "Eisenhower Matrix," which categorizes tasks based on their urgency and importance. Tasks that are both urgent and important should be addressed first, while those that are neither urgent nor important can be deferred or delegated. By practicing this method, children can develop a strategic approach to managing their workload.

Time-blocking is another useful technique for managing time effectively. This involves dividing the day into blocks of time, each dedicated to a specific task or activity. For example, a child might allocate one hour in the afternoon for homework, followed by 30 minutes for a break, and then another hour for extracurricular activities. Time-blocking helps create a structured routine and reduces the likelihood of procrastination by providing clear time frames for each task. It also allows children to focus on one activity at a time, enhancing their concentration and productivity.

Procrastination is a common challenge that can hinder effective time management. Helping children understand the reasons behind procrastination and developing strategies to overcome it is essential. Procrastination often stems from feelings of overwhelm, fear of failure, or a lack of motivation. Encouraging children to start with small, manageable tasks can help them build momentum and gradually tackle more significant challenges. Setting specific deadlines and using positive reinforcement can also motivate children to stay on track. Teaching children to recognize and address procrastination early on fosters a proactive and disciplined approach to managing their time.

Developing a sense of accountability is crucial for successful time management. Children need to take ownership of their responsibilities and understand the consequences of their actions. Encouraging self-reflection and regular check-ins can help children assess their progress and identify areas for improvement. Parents and educators can support this process by providing constructive feedback and guidance. Celebrating successes and acknowledging efforts reinforces positive behaviors and motivates children to continue developing their time management skills.

Balancing different aspects of life is an essential part of time management. Children need to learn how to allocate their time in a way that supports their overall well-being. This includes making time for academics, extracurricular activities, social interactions, and self-care. Encouraging a balanced lifestyle helps children understand the importance of maintaining their physical and mental health while also striving for their goals. Teaching children to recognize the signs of stress and take breaks when needed is vital for preventing burnout and maintaining long-term productivity.

Parents and educators play a significant role in modeling effective time management. Demonstrating organized and disciplined behaviors sets a positive example for children to follow. When children see adults managing their time well, they are more likely to adopt similar habits. Involving children in discussions about time management and sharing personal experiences can provide valuable insights and inspiration. Creating a family or classroom culture that values organization and productivity reinforces the importance of these skills.

Flexibility is an important aspect of time management. While having a structured schedule is beneficial, it is also essential to adapt to unexpected changes and challenges. Teaching children to be flexible and resilient helps them navigate disruptions and adjust their plans accordingly. Encouraging a problem-solving mindset and fostering adaptability ensures that children can handle various situations without becoming overly stressed or discouraged.

Effective time management also involves setting boundaries and saying no when necessary. Children need to learn that they cannot do everything and that it is okay to prioritize their commitments. Teaching children to assess their workload and decline additional tasks when they are already overwhelmed helps prevent overcommitment and stress. Encouraging open communication and providing support in making these decisions fosters a sense of empowerment and self-awareness.

Incorporating mindfulness practices into time management can enhance focus and reduce stress. Techniques such as deep breathing, meditation, and mindful breaks help children stay present and centered, improving their ability to concentrate on tasks. Mindfulness practices also promote self-awareness and emotional regulation, which are essential for managing time effectively. Integrating these practices into daily routines can create a more balanced and productive approach to time management.

Time management skills are not only valuable for academic success but also for personal and professional development. By learning to manage their time effectively, children can achieve a better balance between their responsibilities and personal interests. These skills will serve them well throughout their lives, enabling them to pursue their goals with confidence and resilience. The ability to prioritize, plan, and execute tasks efficiently is a key factor in achieving success and maintaining overall well-being.

In conclusion, developing time management and organizational skills in children is a critical component of their overall development. By understanding the value of time, setting realistic schedules, and using tools and techniques to stay organized, children can build habits that support their productivity and well-being. Teaching prioritization, addressing procrastination, and fostering accountability are essential for effective time management. Balancing different aspects of life, modeling positive behaviors, and maintaining flexibility are key to creating a sustainable and fulfilling approach to managing time. Through intentional guidance and support, parents and educators can empower children to develop the skills and mindset needed to navigate the demands of life with greater ease and efficiency. The benefits of strong time management skills extend far beyond childhood, providing a foundation for success and fulfillment in all areas of life.

ppp

"Family traditions provide continuity and a sense of identity. Celebrating holidays and creating rituals strengthen family bonds. These shared experiences anchor children in their heritage and values."

FOURTEEN

POSITIVE SELF-TALK: BUILDING CONFIDENCE AND RESILIENCE

Positive self-talk is a vital tool in building confidence and resilience in children. It involves guiding children to use affirming and constructive language when thinking or speaking about themselves. The words children use in their internal dialogue significantly impact their self-esteem, emotional health, and overall outlook on life. Teaching positive self-talk helps children develop a growth mindset, cope with challenges, and foster a strong sense of self-worth. The process of cultivating positive self-talk includes understanding its importance, recognizing negative self-talk, replacing it with positive affirmations, and reinforcing these habits through practice and support.

The foundation of positive self-talk begins with helping children understand its importance. Children need to recognize that their thoughts influence their emotions and behaviors. Explaining that positive self-talk can boost their confidence and help them overcome obstacles is a crucial first step. Parents and educators can use simple examples to illustrate this concept, such as comparing how they feel when they say "I can do this" versus "I'm not good at this." By highlighting the difference in feelings and outcomes, children can start to see the power of their words.

Recognizing negative self-talk is the next step in fostering positive self-talk. Children often internalize negative messages from various sources, such as peers, media, or even their own experiences. These negative thoughts can become automatic and pervasive, undermining their self-confidence and resilience. Encouraging children to identify and articulate these negative thoughts is crucial for addressing and transforming them. Parents and educators can help by asking children to share their thoughts when they are feeling upset or discouraged and guiding them to recognize patterns of negative self-talk.

Once negative self-talk is identified, it is important to teach children how to challenge and replace it with positive affirmations. Positive affirmations are simple, positive statements that children can use to counteract negative thoughts and reinforce a positive self-image. For example, if a child frequently thinks, "I can't do anything right," they can replace this thought with, "I am capable, and I can improve with practice." Encouraging children to create a list of positive affirmations tailored to their needs and goals can be a helpful exercise. These affirmations should be realistic, specific, and focused on their strengths and potential.

Practicing positive self-talk consistently is essential for reinforcing these habits. Just like any skill, positive self-talk requires regular practice to become a natural part of a child's thought process. Integrating positive affirmations into daily routines, such as repeating them in the morning or before bedtime, can help solidify this practice. Parents and educators can model positive self-talk by sharing their affirmations and demonstrating how they use them in challenging situations. This modeling reinforces the importance of positive self-talk and provides practical examples for children to follow.

Creating a supportive environment is crucial for fostering positive self-talk. Children thrive in environments where they feel safe, valued, and understood. Encouraging open communication and validating children's feelings helps create a foundation of trust and support. When children express self-doubt or negative thoughts, responding with empathy and encouragement can help them feel heard and supported. Reinforcing positive behavior and celebrating successes, no matter how small, helps build a sense of accomplishment and confidence.

Mindfulness and relaxation techniques can complement the practice of positive self-talk. Mindfulness involves paying attention to the present moment without judgment, which can help children become more aware of their thoughts and feelings. Techniques such as deep breathing, meditation, or guided imagery can help children calm their minds and focus on positive thoughts. These practices promote self-awareness and emotional regulation, making it easier for children to identify and replace negative self-talk with positive affirmations.

Teaching children to set and pursue goals is another effective way to build confidence and resilience through positive self-talk. Setting achievable goals provides children with a sense of purpose and direction. As they work towards these goals, they can use positive self-talk to stay motivated and overcome setbacks. Celebrating their progress and achievements reinforces the value of perseverance and reinforces their belief in their abilities. This process helps children develop a growth mindset, where they see challenges as opportunities for learning and growth rather than as obstacles.

Encouraging children to engage in activities that align with their interests and strengths can also enhance their self-esteem and confidence. When children participate in activities they enjoy and excel in, they are more likely to experience success and feel good about themselves. This positive reinforcement helps build a strong sense of self-worth. Providing opportunities for children to explore different hobbies and interests allows them to discover their passions and develop a diverse set of skills.

Social support is a critical factor in fostering positive self-talk and resilience. Positive relationships with family, friends, and mentors provide a network of support and encouragement. These relationships help children feel connected and valued, boosting their confidence and emotional well-being. Encouraging children to build and maintain positive relationships, participate in group activities, and seek support when needed helps create a strong support system. This network can provide valuable feedback, encouragement, and perspective, helping children navigate challenges and celebrate their successes.

It is also important to address and challenge societal and cultural influences that can contribute to negative self-talk. Children are often exposed to unrealistic standards and negative messages through media and social interactions. These influences can shape their self-perception and lead to harmful comparisons and self-criticism. Educating children about media literacy and encouraging critical thinking helps them recognize and challenge these negative influences. Promoting body positivity, diversity, and acceptance helps create a more inclusive and supportive environment where children can feel confident and valued for who they are.

Building resilience through positive self-talk involves teaching children to view challenges and setbacks as opportunities for growth. Resilience is the ability to bounce back from adversity and continue pursuing goals despite difficulties. Positive self-talk plays a crucial role in fostering resilience by helping children maintain a positive outlook and stay motivated. Encouraging children to reflect on past challenges and identify the strengths and strategies they used to overcome them helps build their confidence and resilience. This reflection reinforces the belief that they have the resources and abilities to handle future challenges.

Creating opportunities for children to take on new challenges and responsibilities can also enhance their resilience and confidence. When children step out of their comfort zones and take on new tasks, they learn to adapt and develop problem-solving skills. Providing support and encouragement during these experiences helps children build confidence and develop a sense of competence. Celebrating their efforts and achievements, regardless of the outcome, reinforces the value of effort and perseverance.

Incorporating positive self-talk into educational settings can also benefit children's academic performance and emotional well-being. Teachers can create a positive classroom environment by encouraging positive self-talk and providing regular feedback and encouragement. Activities such as group discussions, journaling, and reflective exercises can help students practice positive self-talk and develop self-awareness. Integrating social-emotional learning (SEL) into the curriculum helps students develop essential skills such as empathy, self-regulation, and resilience.

It is important to recognize that developing positive self-talk is an ongoing process that requires patience and persistence. Children may encounter setbacks and challenges as they work to change their thought patterns. Providing consistent support and encouragement helps children stay motivated and continue their efforts. Creating a culture that values growth, learning, and self-compassion reinforces the importance of positive self-talk and fosters a positive and supportive environment.

In conclusion, positive self-talk is a powerful tool for building confidence and resilience in children. By guiding children to use affirming and constructive language, parents and educators can help them develop a strong sense of self-worth and the ability to cope with challenges. Understanding the importance of positive self-talk, recognizing and replacing negative self-talk, practicing positive affirmations, and creating a supportive environment are essential steps in fostering these habits. Complementing positive self-talk with mindfulness practices, goal setting, and social support further enhances children's emotional well-being and resilience. Through intentional guidance and practice, children can develop the skills and mindset needed to navigate life's challenges with confidence and resilience, paving the way for a fulfilling and successful future.

ppp

"Gratitude journaling shifts focus from lack to
abundance. Writing down daily thankfulness
fosters a positive perspective. This habit enhances
emotional resilience and joy."

FIFTEEN

SOCIAL SKILLS: FOSTERING FRIENDSHIPS AND COOPERATION

Social skills are essential for fostering friendships and cooperation, playing a crucial role in a child's development and overall well-being. Developing strong social skills helps children build meaningful relationships, navigate social interactions, and work effectively with others. These skills encompass a range of behaviors, including communication, empathy, problem-solving, and cooperation. By nurturing these abilities, parents and educators can equip children with the tools they need to thrive in social settings and form lasting friendships.

Communication is the foundation of social skills. Effective communication involves not only speaking clearly and confidently but also listening actively and empathetically. Teaching children to express themselves in a respectful and articulate manner helps them convey their thoughts and feelings effectively. Encouraging them to use "I" statements, such as "I feel" or "I think," can help them take ownership of their emotions and express themselves without blaming others. Active listening, which involves paying full attention to the speaker, making eye contact, and responding appropriately, is equally important. Teaching children to listen without interrupting and to ask questions for clarification fosters mutual understanding and respect.

Empathy, the ability to understand and share the feelings of others, is another critical component of social skills. Empathetic children are more likely to form strong connections with their peers, as they can relate to and support their friends. Encouraging children to recognize and validate the emotions of others helps them develop empathy. Role-playing activities, where children practice responding to different emotional scenarios, can enhance their ability to empathize. Discussing characters' feelings in books or movies also provides opportunities for children to explore empathy and understand diverse perspectives.

Problem-solving skills are essential for resolving conflicts and maintaining healthy relationships. Teaching children to approach conflicts with a problem-solving mindset helps them address issues constructively. This involves identifying the problem, considering different solutions, and choosing the best course of action. Encouraging children to stay calm, listen to all parties involved, and work together to find a solution promotes cooperation and mutual respect. Parents and educators can model effective problem-solving by demonstrating how to handle disagreements calmly and fairly.

Cooperation, the ability to work together towards a common goal, is a vital social skill that underpins teamwork and collaboration. Cooperative play, such as building a project together or participating in team sports, provides opportunities for children to practice working with others. These activities teach children to share, take turns, and contribute to a group effort. Encouraging cooperative behavior by highlighting the benefits of teamwork and praising collaborative efforts reinforces the value of working together. Group activities and projects in school settings also provide a structured environment for children to develop cooperation skills.

Building friendships requires a combination of these social skills, along with a positive attitude and the ability to connect with others. Teaching children to be friendly, approachable, and open to new experiences helps them form and maintain friendships. Encouraging children to initiate conversations, show interest in others, and be inclusive fosters a welcoming and supportive social environment. Teaching children to recognize and respect boundaries, both their own and others', is also important for healthy relationships. Respecting personal space, asking for consent, and being mindful of others' comfort levels are essential aspects of social interactions.

Developing social skills also involves teaching children about social norms and expectations. Understanding appropriate behavior in different social contexts helps children navigate various situations confidently. This includes learning about manners, such as saying "please" and "thank you," making polite introductions, and being considerate of others. Parents and educators can reinforce these norms by modeling respectful behavior and providing gentle reminders when needed. Social stories, which are narratives that describe social situations and appropriate responses, can be a helpful tool for teaching social norms.

Social skills development can be supported through structured activities and unstructured play. Structured activities, such as group projects, games, and sports, provide opportunities for children to practice specific social skills in a guided environment. These activities often involve rules and objectives that require cooperation, communication, and problem-solving. Unstructured play, on the other hand, allows children to explore social interactions more freely and creatively. Both types of play are important for well-rounded social development, as they offer different ways for children to engage with peers and practice social skills.

Parents and educators play a crucial role in fostering social skills by creating supportive and inclusive environments. Providing opportunities for children to interact with diverse groups helps them learn about different cultures, perspectives, and ways of thinking. Encouraging children to participate in community activities, such as clubs, sports teams, or volunteer projects, exposes them to new social experiences and helps them build a broader network of friends. Inclusive environments where all children feel valued and respected promote a sense of belonging and encourage positive social interactions.

Modeling positive social behavior is one of the most effective ways to teach social skills. Children learn by observing the actions and attitudes of the adults around them. Demonstrating kindness, empathy, and effective communication sets a positive example for children to follow. Parents and educators can also share their own experiences with building friendships and cooperating with others, providing practical insights and advice. Creating opportunities for children to observe and participate in positive social interactions helps reinforce these behaviors.

Encouraging children to reflect on their social interactions and experiences can enhance their social skills. Discussing what went well and what could be improved helps children develop self-awareness and learn from their experiences. Reflective questions, such as "How did you feel during that interaction?" or "What would you do differently next time?" can prompt meaningful conversations and insights. Journaling or drawing about social experiences can also be a helpful way for children to process their thoughts and feelings.

Developing social skills is a continuous process that evolves as children grow and face new social challenges. Providing ongoing support and guidance helps children navigate these changes and continue developing their social abilities. Parents and educators can offer reassurance and encouragement, helping children build confidence in their social skills. Positive reinforcement, such as praising specific behaviors or acknowledging efforts to improve, motivates children to keep practicing and refining their skills.

For children who struggle with social interactions, additional support and interventions may be needed. Social skills groups, where children can practice social interactions in a structured and supportive environment, can be beneficial. These groups often use role-playing, games, and discussions to teach and reinforce social skills. Working with a counselor or therapist can also provide individualized support for children who need extra help with social development. It is important to approach these interventions with empathy and patience, recognizing that social skills development can be challenging for some children.

Technology can also play a role in social skills development, both positively and negatively. On the positive side, technology can provide platforms for children to connect with others, share interests, and practice communication. Online games, social media, and virtual learning environments offer new ways for children to interact and collaborate. However, it is important to monitor and guide children's use of technology to ensure that it supports positive social interactions and does not lead to negative behaviors, such as cyberbullying or excessive screen time. Encouraging a balanced approach to technology use, where online interactions complement face-to-face social experiences, helps children develop a well-rounded set of social skills.

Ultimately, fostering social skills in children is about helping them build the confidence and competence to navigate social interactions with ease and grace. By teaching communication, empathy, problem-solving, and cooperation, parents and educators can equip children with the tools they need to form meaningful friendships and work effectively with others. Creating supportive and inclusive environments, modeling positive behavior, and providing opportunities for practice and reflection are key strategies for promoting social skills development. Through intentional guidance and support, children can develop the social skills that will enable them to thrive in their relationships and contribute positively to their communities. These skills will serve them well throughout their lives, enhancing their personal and professional success and overall well-being.

◁◁◁

"Effective communication in the family fosters understanding and empathy. Open conversations about thoughts and feelings build trust. This practice strengthens relationships and supports emotional health."

SIXTEEN
GRATITUDE PRACTICE: NURTURING APPRECIATION

Gratitude practice is an essential aspect of nurturing appreciation in children, fostering a positive mindset that can significantly enhance their emotional well-being and overall happiness. Teaching children to recognize and express gratitude helps them develop a deeper appreciation for the people, experiences, and things in their lives. This practice not only promotes positive relationships and emotional health but also builds resilience and a sense of contentment. Integrating gratitude into daily routines and creating opportunities for children to practice thankfulness can cultivate a lifelong habit of appreciation.

The first step in fostering gratitude is helping children understand what it means to be grateful. Gratitude involves recognizing the good things in life and acknowledging the efforts and kindness of others. It is about focusing on what one has rather than what one lacks. Parents and educators can introduce the concept of gratitude through discussions and examples, explaining that being grateful means appreciating the small and big things that bring joy and comfort. These conversations can highlight that gratitude is not just about saying "thank you" but about truly feeling and expressing appreciation.

One effective way to nurture gratitude is by incorporating gratitude practices into daily routines. Simple activities such as keeping a gratitude journal can help children develop the habit of reflecting on their blessings. Encouraging children to write down three things they are grateful for each day can shift their focus towards positivity and help them recognize the abundance in their lives. This practice can be done in the morning to set a positive tone for the day or in the evening as a way to end the day on a thankful note. For younger children who may not yet write fluently, drawing pictures or sharing gratitude verbally can be just as effective.

Gratitude can also be practiced through family rituals and traditions. Setting aside time during meals, such as dinner, for family members to share what they are grateful for can create a sense of connection and mutual appreciation. This practice not only fosters gratitude but also strengthens family bonds and encourages open communication. Special occasions like birthdays or holidays can be opportunities to express gratitude for family and friends, emphasizing the importance of relationships and shared experiences.

Acts of kindness and generosity are another powerful way to nurture gratitude. When children engage in acts of kindness, they learn to appreciate the positive impact they can have on others. Volunteering as a family, helping a neighbor, or participating in community service projects can provide meaningful experiences that highlight the value of giving and receiving. These activities teach children that gratitude is not just about what they receive but also about what they can give. Encouraging children to perform random acts of kindness, such as writing thank-you notes, helping a classmate, or donating toys, reinforces the connection between gratitude and generosity.

Mindfulness practices can complement gratitude by helping children become more aware of the present moment and the positive aspects of their lives. Mindfulness involves paying attention to the here and now with an open and non-judgmental attitude. Teaching children mindfulness techniques such as deep breathing, meditation, or guided imagery can help them focus on the good things around them. A mindful walk in nature, where children pay attention to the sights, sounds, and smells, can enhance their sense of appreciation for the natural world. Integrating mindfulness with gratitude practices, such as a gratitude meditation where children focus on the things they are thankful for, can deepen their sense of appreciation.

Storytelling and reading books that emphasize gratitude can also be effective in nurturing appreciation. Stories that highlight characters who express thankfulness or learn the importance of gratitude can provide relatable examples for children. Discussing these stories and exploring the characters' experiences can help children understand the value of gratitude in different contexts. Parents and educators can also share personal stories of gratitude, modeling how to recognize and express thankfulness in everyday life.

Creating a gratitude jar is a fun and interactive way for children to practice gratitude. Family members can write down things they are grateful for on slips of paper and place them in the jar. Over time, the jar fills up with positive memories and moments of appreciation. Reviewing the contents of the jar together, especially during challenging times, can remind children of the good things in their lives and reinforce a positive mindset. This activity can be adapted for individual use, where children keep their own gratitude jar and add to it regularly.

Gratitude practices can be integrated into educational settings as well. Teachers can incorporate gratitude activities into the classroom routine, such as starting the day with a gratitude circle where students share what they are thankful for. Writing assignments that focus on gratitude, such as letters of thanks to people who have made a difference in their lives, can help students articulate and express their appreciation. Classroom projects that involve community service or acts of kindness can also promote gratitude and a sense of social responsibility.

Gratitude is closely linked to positive psychology and the concept of a growth mindset. Teaching children that they can develop their abilities and overcome challenges through effort and perseverance can foster a sense of gratitude for their opportunities and experiences. Encouraging a growth mindset involves praising effort rather than innate talent and emphasizing the learning process over the outcome. This approach helps children appreciate their own progress and resilience, fostering a sense of gratitude for their personal growth.

It is important to address and challenge the barriers to gratitude that children may encounter. In a consumer-driven society, children are often exposed to messages that emphasize materialism and instant gratification. Teaching children to appreciate what they have rather than constantly seeking more requires conscious effort. Discussions about the difference between needs and wants, and the value of non-material blessings such as relationships, health, and experiences, can help shift their focus. Limiting exposure to advertising and promoting experiences over possessions can also support a more gratitude-focused mindset.

Gratitude practices can also be tailored to individual preferences and needs. Some children may prefer writing in a journal, while others might enjoy expressing gratitude through art or verbal communication. Providing a variety of options allows children to choose the method that resonates with them, making the practice more meaningful and sustainable. Encouraging children to explore different ways of expressing gratitude helps them find what works best for them and reinforces the habit.

Modeling gratitude is one of the most effective ways to teach it. Children learn by observing the behaviors and attitudes of the adults around them. When parents and educators consistently demonstrate gratitude, whether through words or actions, children are more likely to adopt these behaviors. Expressing gratitude openly, such as thanking others, acknowledging small acts of kindness, and showing appreciation for everyday moments, sets a positive example. Sharing personal experiences of gratitude and discussing how they impact one's life can also provide valuable insights.

Reflecting on the benefits of gratitude can reinforce its importance and motivate children to continue practicing it. Gratitude has been shown to enhance emotional well-being, improve relationships, and increase overall life satisfaction. Discussing these benefits with children and helping them recognize how gratitude positively affects their lives can encourage them to embrace the practice. Encouraging children to notice how they feel after expressing or experiencing gratitude can deepen their understanding of its impact.

It is important to approach gratitude practices with authenticity and sincerity. Forced or insincere expressions of gratitude can be counterproductive and may lead to resistance. Encouraging genuine gratitude involves helping children recognize and appreciate what they truly feel thankful for, rather than what they think they should be thankful for. Allowing children to express gratitude in their own way and at their own pace fosters a more authentic and meaningful practice.

In conclusion, gratitude practice is a powerful tool for nurturing appreciation and fostering a positive mindset in children. By helping children understand the concept of gratitude, incorporating it into daily routines, and creating opportunities for thankfulness, parents and educators can cultivate a habit of appreciation. Practices such as gratitude journaling, family rituals, acts of kindness, mindfulness, storytelling, and creative activities can all contribute to a deeper sense of gratitude. Addressing barriers to gratitude and providing a supportive environment further enhances the practice. Through consistent modeling, reflection, and authentic expression, children can develop a lifelong habit of gratitude that enhances their emotional well-being and overall happiness. The benefits of gratitude extend far beyond individual well-being, promoting positive relationships, resilience, and a greater sense of contentment and fulfillment in life.

ppp

"Encouraging artistic habits nurtures creativity and self-expression. Providing diverse materials and opportunities for exploration empowers children. This environment fosters innovation and critical thinking."

SEVENTEEN

CREATIVE EXPRESSION: ENCOURAGING ARTISTIC HABITS

Creative expression is a vital aspect of human development, and encouraging artistic habits in children can have profound effects on their growth and well-being. Artistic activities provide children with a unique outlet for self-expression, allowing them to communicate their thoughts, emotions, and ideas in ways that words may not always capture. Fostering creative expression helps children develop critical thinking, problem-solving skills, and emotional intelligence. It also promotes confidence, resilience, and a sense of accomplishment. By creating an environment that supports and encourages artistic habits, parents and educators can help children explore their creativity and cultivate a lifelong appreciation for the arts.

The foundation of encouraging artistic habits in children begins with providing opportunities for exploration. Children should have access to a variety of materials and mediums to experiment with, such as crayons, paints, clay, musical instruments, and dance spaces. This exposure allows them to discover their preferences and interests, whether it be drawing, painting, sculpture, music, dance, or drama. Allowing children to choose their artistic activities gives them a sense of ownership and autonomy, fostering a deeper connection to their creative endeavors.

Encouraging a process-oriented approach to art rather than focusing solely on the end product is crucial. Children should feel free to explore and experiment without the pressure of producing something perfect or meeting specific standards. Emphasizing the joy of creation and the experience of making art helps children develop a positive attitude towards their artistic pursuits. This approach also reduces fear of failure and encourages risk-taking, which are essential components of creativity. Praising the effort and the creative process rather than the final outcome reinforces the value of artistic exploration.

Providing a supportive and nurturing environment is key to fostering artistic habits. Children need to feel that their creative efforts are valued and appreciated. Displaying their artwork at home or in the classroom shows that their creativity is important and worthy of recognition. Creating a dedicated space for artistic activities, whether it be a corner of a room or a specific table, signals to children that their creative expression is a priority. This space should be well-stocked with a variety of materials and tools, making it easy for children to engage in artistic activities whenever inspiration strikes.

Encouraging artistic habits also involves integrating creativity into daily routines. Regular time for creative activities can be incorporated into the schedule, much like reading or homework. This routine helps children develop a habit of engaging with their creativity regularly. Parents and educators can participate in artistic activities alongside children, making it a shared experience that strengthens bonds and provides additional encouragement. Collaborative projects, such as family art nights or group performances, can further enhance the sense of community and shared creative expression.

Exposure to diverse forms of art and culture is another important aspect of encouraging artistic habits. Taking children to museums, galleries, theater performances, concerts, and cultural festivals broadens their horizons and exposes them to different artistic expressions. These experiences can inspire children and provide new ideas and perspectives for their own creative work. Discussing the art they see and encouraging them to reflect on their experiences fosters critical thinking and deeper engagement with the arts.

Integrating art with other areas of learning can also enhance creative expression. For example, incorporating drawing or storytelling into subjects like science, history, or language arts can make learning more engaging and help children make connections between different disciplines. Artistic activities can be used to reinforce concepts, such as creating dioramas for history lessons or composing songs to remember mathematical formulas. This interdisciplinary approach shows children that creativity is not confined to the arts but is a valuable skill that can enhance all areas of learning.

Encouraging creative expression also means allowing children to experience and process a wide range of emotions through their art. Artistic activities provide a safe space for children to explore and express their feelings, whether they are joy, sadness, anger, or confusion. Parents and educators can support this emotional exploration by being open and non-judgmental about the emotions expressed in children's artwork. Asking open-ended questions about their creations, such as "What were you thinking about when you made this?" or "How does this piece make you feel?" can encourage children to articulate their emotions and thoughts, promoting emotional intelligence and self-awareness.

Feedback and constructive criticism are essential for artistic growth, but they should be delivered in a way that is supportive and encouraging. Rather than focusing on what might be wrong with a piece of art, parents and educators can highlight what works well and suggest ways to further develop certain aspects. Encouraging children to reflect on their own work and identify areas they are proud of, as well as areas they want to improve, fosters a growth mindset and a sense of ownership over their creative process.

Artistic expression is not limited to traditional visual arts but includes performing arts such as music, dance, and theater. Encouraging children to explore these forms of creative expression can provide them with different ways to communicate and express themselves. Music lessons, dance classes, or participation in theater productions can help children develop discipline, confidence, and teamwork skills. These activities also provide opportunities for public performance, which can boost self-esteem and resilience.

Incorporating technology into artistic activities can also expand the possibilities for creative expression. Digital art, animation, music production, and video editing are just a few examples of how technology can enhance artistic endeavors. Providing children with access to digital tools and teaching them how to use these technologies can open up new avenues for creativity. Encouraging children to blend traditional and digital art forms can lead to innovative and unique creations.

Parents and educators can further support artistic development by being actively involved in the arts themselves. When children see the adults in their lives engaging in creative activities, they are more likely to value and pursue their own artistic interests. Sharing artistic experiences, such as attending a concert together or working on a craft project, can inspire children and show them that creativity is a lifelong pursuit. Demonstrating enthusiasm for the arts and celebrating creativity in all its forms helps create a culture that values and supports artistic expression.

It is important to recognize and celebrate the diverse ways in which children express their creativity. Every child is unique, and their creative interests and talents may vary widely. Providing opportunities for all types of artistic expression, whether it be drawing, dancing, writing, or building, ensures that every child can find a way to connect with their creativity. Celebrating and respecting this diversity fosters an inclusive environment where all forms of artistic expression are valued.

Encouraging artistic habits also involves teaching children about the artistic process and the effort that goes into creating art. Understanding that creativity often involves trial and error, experimentation, and persistence helps children develop resilience and patience. Discussing the creative process of various artists, whether through biographies, documentaries, or guest speakers, can provide valuable insights and inspiration. This understanding helps children appreciate the journey of creating art and the dedication required to develop their skills.

Ultimately, fostering creative expression in children is about providing them with the tools, opportunities, and support to explore and develop their artistic talents. It is about creating an environment that values creativity and encourages children to express themselves freely and authentically. By integrating artistic activities into daily routines, providing diverse experiences, and celebrating all forms of creativity, parents and educators can help children develop a lifelong appreciation for the arts. This appreciation not only enriches their own lives but also contributes to a more vibrant and creative society. Through intentional support and encouragement, children can discover the joy and fulfillment that comes from creative expression, building a foundation for personal growth and artistic achievement.

❦❦❦

"Collaborative activities teach the value of teamwork. Group projects and sports promote cooperation and mutual respect. These experiences build social skills and a sense of community."

EIGHTEEN

PROBLEM-SOLVING: DEVELOPING CRITICAL THINKING

Problem-solving is an essential skill that plays a crucial role in developing critical thinking. It enables individuals to navigate challenges, make informed decisions, and innovate solutions. Developing these skills in children from an early age sets the foundation for their academic success, personal growth, and future professional achievements. Effective problem-solving involves identifying and understanding the problem, generating potential solutions, evaluating and selecting the best solution, and implementing and reflecting on the outcome. By fostering these abilities, parents and educators can help children become confident, independent thinkers capable of addressing complex issues.

The first step in problem-solving is recognizing and defining the problem clearly. Children need to learn how to observe situations, identify discrepancies or difficulties, and articulate these issues precisely. Teaching children to ask questions like "What is the problem?" and "Why is this a problem?" helps them develop a clear understanding of the challenge they are facing. This process involves breaking down the problem into smaller, more manageable parts, which makes it easier to analyze and address. Encouraging children to describe the problem in their own words reinforces their comprehension and helps them internalize the first step of problem-solving.

Once the problem is clearly defined, the next step is generating a range of potential solutions. Brainstorming is a valuable technique for this phase, as it encourages creativity and open-mindedness. Children should be encouraged to think freely and come up with as many ideas as possible without immediate judgment or evaluation. This approach fosters a sense of possibility and innovation, allowing children to explore a variety of options. Techniques such as mind mapping or listing can help organize and visualize their ideas, making it easier to compare and contrast different solutions.

Evaluating potential solutions is a critical aspect of problem-solving that requires analytical thinking. Children need to learn how to assess the feasibility, effectiveness, and potential consequences of each option. This involves considering the pros and cons, predicting possible outcomes, and weighing the advantages and disadvantages. Teaching children to ask questions such as "What are the benefits of this solution?" and "What challenges might arise from this choice?" helps them develop a balanced and thorough approach to evaluation. Role-playing different scenarios can also be an effective way to explore the implications of various solutions and gain deeper insights.

Selecting the best solution involves making informed decisions based on the evaluation process. Children should be guided to choose the option that best addresses the problem while considering practical constraints and available resources. This step often requires prioritizing certain criteria, such as efficiency, cost, or time, depending on the context of the problem. Encouraging children to explain their reasoning and justify their choices helps solidify their decision-making skills and promotes accountability. This practice also reinforces their ability to think critically and logically.

Implementing the chosen solution is where children put their plans into action. This step involves practical execution and often requires flexibility and adaptability. Children need to be prepared for potential obstacles and be ready to adjust their approach if necessary. Monitoring progress and making necessary adjustments are crucial components of successful implementation. Teaching children to stay focused and persistent while being open to feedback and change helps them navigate the implementation phase effectively. Parents and educators can support this process by providing guidance, resources, and encouragement.

Reflecting on the outcome is a vital part of the problem-solving process that promotes continuous learning and improvement. After implementing a solution, children should evaluate its effectiveness and consider what worked well and what could be improved. This reflection helps them understand the impact of their decisions and actions, reinforcing their learning and preparing them for future challenges. Encouraging children to ask reflective questions such as "What did I learn from this experience?" and "How can I apply this learning to future problems?" fosters a growth mindset and a commitment to ongoing development.

Developing critical thinking through problem-solving also involves fostering a mindset that values curiosity, skepticism, and open-mindedness. Children should be encouraged to question assumptions, seek out new information, and consider multiple perspectives. This mindset helps them approach problems with a sense of inquiry and a willingness to explore different possibilities. Engaging in activities that challenge their thinking, such as puzzles, games, and debates, can stimulate their intellectual curiosity and enhance their critical thinking skills.

Collaboration and communication are integral to effective problem-solving. Working with others allows children to share ideas, gain different viewpoints, and leverage collective knowledge and skills. Teaching children how to communicate effectively, listen actively, and work cooperatively with others enhances their ability to solve problems collaboratively. Group projects, team-based activities, and discussions provide opportunities for children to practice these skills in a supportive environment. Collaboration also fosters social and emotional development, as children learn to navigate interpersonal dynamics and build positive relationships.

Encouraging a hands-on, experiential approach to learning can significantly enhance problem-solving and critical thinking skills. Activities such as science experiments, engineering projects, and real-world problem-solving scenarios provide practical experiences that reinforce theoretical knowledge. These activities help children apply what they have learned in meaningful ways, deepening their understanding and building their confidence in their abilities. Experiential learning also promotes resilience and adaptability, as children encounter and overcome real challenges.

Parents and educators play a crucial role in modeling effective problem-solving and critical thinking behaviors. Demonstrating how to approach problems thoughtfully, make decisions based on evidence, and reflect on outcomes sets a positive example for children. Sharing personal experiences and discussing the reasoning behind decisions can provide valuable insights and inspiration. Creating an environment that values and encourages critical thinking, inquiry, and reflection reinforces these behaviors and supports children's development.

Integrating problem-solving and critical thinking into the curriculum can enhance students' engagement and learning outcomes. Project-based learning, inquiry-based learning, and interdisciplinary approaches provide opportunities for students to tackle complex problems and develop their critical thinking skills. These methods encourage students to apply knowledge from different subjects, think creatively, and work collaboratively. Providing real-world contexts and challenges makes learning more relevant and meaningful, motivating students to engage deeply with the material.

Technology can also be a valuable tool for enhancing problem-solving and critical thinking skills. Digital resources, such as educational apps, simulations, and online collaborative platforms, offer interactive and engaging ways for children to explore problems and develop solutions. Technology can provide access to a wealth of information and tools that support research, analysis, and experimentation. Integrating technology thoughtfully into problem-solving activities can enhance learning and provide new opportunities for innovation and creativity.

Encouraging self-reflection and self-assessment helps children develop a deeper understanding of their problem-solving processes and critical thinking skills. Reflective practices, such as journaling, self-assessment checklists, and peer feedback, promote self-awareness and continuous improvement. Encouraging children to set personal goals for their development and track their progress reinforces their commitment to growth and learning. Self-reflection also helps children recognize their strengths and areas for improvement, guiding their future efforts and building their confidence.

Resilience and adaptability are essential qualities for effective problem-solving and critical thinking. Children need to learn how to cope with setbacks, persevere through challenges, and remain flexible in their thinking. Teaching strategies for managing stress, staying motivated, and maintaining a positive attitude helps children build resilience. Encouraging a growth mindset, where children view challenges as opportunities for learning and development, fosters adaptability and a proactive approach to problem-solving.

In conclusion, problem-solving and critical thinking are essential skills that enable children to navigate complex challenges, make informed decisions, and innovate solutions. By teaching children to identify and define problems, generate and evaluate potential solutions, implement and reflect on outcomes, and develop a mindset that values inquiry and open-mindedness, parents and educators can equip them with the tools they need for success. Collaboration, communication, experiential learning, and technology integration further enhance these skills, providing opportunities for practical application and continuous growth. Through intentional guidance and support, children can develop into confident, independent thinkers capable of addressing the challenges of today and tomorrow with creativity and resilience.

ppp

"Teaching children to set realistic goals fosters a growth mindset. Celebrating their efforts and achievements, no matter how small, builds confidence. This approach emphasizes the importance of perseverance and progress."

NINETEEN
Family Time: Strengthening Bonds and Traditions

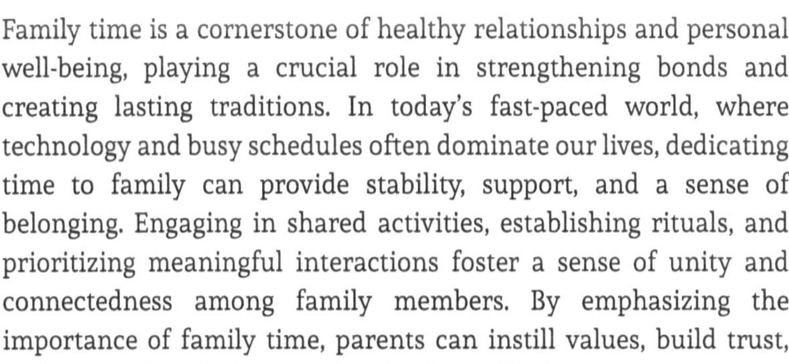

Family time is a cornerstone of healthy relationships and personal well-being, playing a crucial role in strengthening bonds and creating lasting traditions. In today's fast-paced world, where technology and busy schedules often dominate our lives, dedicating time to family can provide stability, support, and a sense of belonging. Engaging in shared activities, establishing rituals, and prioritizing meaningful interactions foster a sense of unity and connectedness among family members. By emphasizing the importance of family time, parents can instill values, build trust, and create cherished memories that last a lifetime.

One of the most significant benefits of family time is the opportunity it provides for open communication. Regular, uninterrupted time together allows family members to discuss their thoughts, feelings, and experiences, fostering understanding and empathy. This communication is vital for addressing conflicts, sharing joys, and supporting each other through challenges. Parents can model effective communication by actively listening to their children, validating their feelings, and encouraging open dialogue. Creating an environment where everyone feels heard and respected strengthens the emotional bonds within the family.

Shared activities, such as playing games, cooking meals, or embarking on outdoor adventures, can also enhance family cohesion. These activities provide opportunities for collaboration, teamwork, and mutual enjoyment. Engaging in fun and relaxing activities together helps reduce stress and creates a sense of unity and happiness. Simple actions like having dinner together every night or planning a weekly family game night can have a profound impact on family dynamics. These shared experiences become the foundation of family traditions, providing continuity and a sense of identity.

Family traditions play a crucial role in creating a sense of belonging and continuity. Traditions, whether they are holiday celebrations, annual vacations, or weekly rituals, provide a framework for family life that is predictable and comforting. These rituals help children understand their family's values and history, fostering a sense of pride and connection. Establishing and maintaining traditions require intentional effort, but the rewards are significant. For example, celebrating holidays with specific customs, such as decorating the house, preparing special meals, or participating in community events, can create lasting memories and a sense of continuity across generations.

In addition to established traditions, families can create new rituals that reflect their evolving interests and values. These can be as simple as a Sunday morning walk in the park, a monthly movie night, or a yearly camping trip. Creating new traditions allows families to adapt to changes and stay connected in meaningful ways. Involving children in the planning and decision-making process for these activities can make them feel valued and included, reinforcing their sense of belonging and importance within the family unit.

Family time is also an opportunity to teach and reinforce important life skills and values. Through shared activities, parents can impart lessons on cooperation, responsibility, and respect. For example, cooking together can teach children about nutrition, following instructions, and working as a team. Family meetings can provide a forum for discussing goals, responsibilities, and problem-solving strategies, teaching children how to communicate effectively and make decisions collaboratively. By engaging in these activities, parents can instill values such as honesty, integrity, and kindness, shaping their children's character and guiding their development.

Moreover, family time contributes significantly to the emotional and psychological well-being of all family members. Children who feel connected to their families are more likely to have higher self-esteem, better academic performance, and stronger social skills. The sense of security and support that comes from strong family bonds helps children navigate the challenges of growing up with confidence and resilience. For parents, spending quality time with their children provides a sense of fulfillment and strengthens the parent-child relationship, fostering mutual respect and affection.

In today's digital age, managing technology use is a crucial aspect of maintaining quality family time. While technology can offer opportunities for bonding, such as playing video games together or watching a family movie, it can also create distractions that hinder meaningful interactions. Setting boundaries around technology use, such as designated screen-free times or areas, can help ensure that family time remains focused and connected. Encouraging activities that do not involve screens, such as board games, outdoor sports, or creative projects, can promote more engaging and interactive family experiences.

Family time is also an opportunity to celebrate each other's achievements and milestones. Acknowledging and celebrating accomplishments, whether big or small, reinforces a sense of pride and support within the family. These celebrations can range from throwing a party for a significant achievement to simply acknowledging a job well done during a family meal. Recognizing each other's efforts and successes fosters a positive and encouraging family environment, where everyone feels valued and appreciated.

In addition to planned activities and traditions, spontaneous moments of connection are equally important. These unplanned interactions, such as a heartfelt conversation during a car ride or a shared laugh over a funny incident, contribute to the overall fabric of family life. Being present and attentive to these opportunities for connection helps build a strong and resilient family bond. Parents can encourage these moments by being available and responsive to their children's needs and by creating an atmosphere where spontaneous interactions are welcomed and cherished.

Balancing family time with individual needs and activities is also important. While spending time together strengthens family bonds, it is equally important for family members to have time for themselves and their personal interests. Encouraging individual hobbies and activities allows each person to develop their own identity and skills, which can enrich the family dynamic. Supporting each other's interests and providing space for individual growth fosters a healthy balance between togetherness and independence.

Family time can also include extended family members, such as grandparents, aunts, uncles, and cousins. Maintaining connections with extended family members provides a broader support network and helps children understand their family history and heritage. Family gatherings, reunions, and visits can strengthen these bonds and create a sense of belonging within a larger family context. These interactions also offer opportunities for children to learn from and be influenced by a variety of family members, each bringing their own experiences and perspectives.

Incorporating acts of service and community involvement into family time can also strengthen family bonds and instill values of compassion and social responsibility. Volunteering together for a local charity, participating in community clean-up events, or supporting a cause as a family can provide meaningful and fulfilling experiences. These activities not only strengthen family unity but also teach children the importance of giving back and being active, responsible members of their community.

In conclusion, family time is an essential aspect of building strong, healthy relationships and creating lasting traditions. By prioritizing meaningful interactions, shared activities, and open communication, families can foster a sense of unity, support, and belonging. Establishing and maintaining traditions, managing technology use, and balancing family time with individual needs contribute to a positive and nurturing family environment. Through intentional effort and a commitment to spending quality time together, families can create cherished memories, instill important values, and strengthen the bonds that hold them together. The benefits of family time extend far beyond the immediate moments of connection, providing a foundation of love, support, and resilience that lasts a lifetime.

ϷϷϷ

"Balancing technology use with meaningful family time strengthens relationships. Shared, screen-free activities enhance connection and communication. This balance fosters a supportive and engaging family environment."

TWENTY

HABIT TRACKING: CELEBRATING PROGRESS AND GROWTH

Habit tracking is a powerful tool for celebrating progress and growth. It involves monitoring and recording specific actions or behaviors to cultivate positive habits and achieve long-term goals. By visually tracking habits, individuals can gain insights into their behaviors, maintain motivation, and recognize their accomplishments. This practice can be especially beneficial for children, helping them develop discipline, responsibility, and a sense of achievement. Habit tracking encourages consistency and perseverance, fostering a growth mindset and reinforcing the importance of incremental progress. Through intentional tracking and regular reflection, individuals can celebrate their journey and build a foundation for sustained personal growth.

The process of habit tracking begins with identifying the habits or goals to be monitored. These can range from daily routines such as brushing teeth, reading, or exercising, to more specific targets like completing homework, practicing a musical instrument, or drinking a certain amount of water. It is important to start with clear and achievable goals that are meaningful and relevant to the individual. By focusing on specific actions, habit tracking provides a concrete way to measure progress and maintain accountability.

Once the goals are defined, selecting an appropriate tracking method is crucial. There are various tools and techniques available for habit tracking, including digital apps, paper journals, and visual charts. Digital apps offer features such as reminders, progress charts, and motivational quotes, making it easy to track habits on-the-go. Paper journals or planners provide a tactile and customizable option, allowing for creativity and personal expression. Visual charts, such as habit trackers or calendars, offer a simple and effective way to see progress at a glance. Choosing a method that aligns with the individual's preferences and lifestyle increases the likelihood of consistent tracking.

Consistency is key to effective habit tracking. Recording progress daily or at regular intervals helps reinforce the habit and provides ongoing motivation. By making habit tracking a routine part of the day, individuals can integrate it seamlessly into their lives. For children, incorporating habit tracking into their morning or evening routines can create a structured and predictable system. Parents and educators can support this process by setting aside dedicated time for tracking and providing gentle reminders as needed. Establishing a regular tracking schedule helps build momentum and fosters a sense of commitment.

Celebrating small wins is an essential aspect of habit tracking. Recognizing and rewarding progress, no matter how minor, boosts motivation and reinforces positive behaviors. Celebrations can take various forms, from verbal praise and high-fives to tangible rewards like stickers or small treats. For children, creating a reward system that acknowledges their efforts and achievements can be highly motivating. For example, earning a sticker for each day a habit is completed and exchanging a certain number of stickers for a reward can provide a fun and engaging incentive. Celebrating progress emphasizes the value of consistency and perseverance, encouraging continued effort.

Reflecting on progress and setbacks is a vital part of the habit tracking process. Regular reflection helps individuals understand their patterns, identify challenges, and make necessary adjustments. By reviewing their tracking records, individuals can see trends and gain insights into what strategies work best for them. Reflecting on setbacks or missed days with a growth mindset fosters resilience and adaptability. Instead of viewing setbacks as failures, individuals can see them as opportunities to learn and improve. Encouraging children to reflect on their progress and discuss their experiences promotes self-awareness and critical thinking.

Visualizing progress through habit tracking charts or graphs provides a tangible representation of growth. Seeing a visual record of consistent effort can be highly motivating and satisfying. Visual trackers, such as colored-in charts or marked calendars, offer a clear and immediate way to see progress. These visual cues serve as constant reminders of the individual's commitment and achievements. For children, creating colorful and interactive trackers can make the process more engaging and enjoyable. Displaying the trackers in a visible location, such as a bedroom wall or a classroom, reinforces the habit and serves as a source of pride.

Accountability is another important aspect of habit tracking. Sharing goals and progress with others can provide additional motivation and support. For children, involving parents, teachers, or peers in the tracking process can create a sense of accountability and encouragement. Regular check-ins or progress updates with a trusted person can help maintain focus and commitment. For example, parents can review the habit tracker with their child each week, celebrating successes and discussing any challenges. This collaborative approach fosters a supportive environment where the individual feels encouraged and valued.

Habit tracking can also be integrated into educational settings to support students' academic and personal development. Teachers can use habit trackers to help students develop positive study habits, time management skills, and healthy routines. Classroom habit trackers can encourage collective goals, such as reading a certain number of books or practicing kindness. These collective goals promote teamwork and a sense of community, reinforcing positive behaviors in a group setting. Educators can provide regular feedback and recognition, creating a positive and motivating learning environment.

Technology offers various tools and resources for habit tracking, making it accessible and convenient. Digital habit tracking apps provide features such as reminders, progress graphs, and motivational quotes, enhancing the tracking experience. These apps can be customized to suit individual preferences and goals, offering a personalized approach to habit tracking. For children, using apps with interactive and gamified elements can make the process fun and engaging. Parents and educators can explore different apps to find the ones that best support the individual's needs and preferences.

The benefits of habit tracking extend beyond achieving specific goals. By developing the practice of habit tracking, individuals cultivate important life skills such as self-discipline, perseverance, and time management. Tracking habits reinforces the idea that small, consistent actions lead to significant progress over time. This mindset fosters a sense of empowerment and self-efficacy, as individuals see their efforts translate into tangible results. For children, habit tracking provides a structured way to develop these skills, building a foundation for future success.

In addition to individual habits, tracking collective goals can foster a sense of teamwork and shared achievement. Families, classrooms, or groups can set common goals and track their progress together. Collective habit tracking encourages collaboration, mutual support, and accountability. Celebrating collective achievements reinforces the value of teamwork and strengthens social bonds. For example, a family might track their progress towards a shared goal, such as reducing screen time or increasing physical activity, and celebrate their success with a special outing or activity.

Mindfulness and self-reflection are integral components of effective habit tracking. By paying attention to their behaviors and reflecting on their progress, individuals develop greater self-awareness and intentionality. Habit tracking encourages individuals to be present and mindful of their actions, fostering a deeper connection to their goals. For children, incorporating mindfulness practices such as deep breathing or journaling into the tracking process can enhance their self-awareness and emotional regulation. Mindful habit tracking promotes a holistic approach to personal growth, integrating physical, mental, and emotional well-being.

Flexibility and adaptability are important qualities in the habit tracking process. While consistency is key, it is also important to be adaptable and responsive to changing circumstances. Life events, challenges, or shifts in priorities may require adjustments to goals or tracking methods. Encouraging a flexible mindset helps individuals navigate these changes without losing motivation. For children, teaching them to adapt their habits and tracking methods as needed fosters resilience and problem-solving skills. Emphasizing progress over perfection reinforces the idea that growth is a dynamic and ongoing process.

In conclusion, habit tracking is a powerful and effective tool for celebrating progress and fostering personal growth. By identifying specific goals, selecting appropriate tracking methods, and maintaining consistency, individuals can develop positive habits and achieve their objectives. Celebrating small wins, reflecting on progress, and visualizing growth enhance motivation and reinforce positive behaviors. Accountability, both individual and collective, provides additional support and encouragement. Integrating habit tracking into daily routines, educational settings, and family activities creates a structured and supportive environment for personal development. Through intentional practice and mindfulness, habit tracking cultivates important life skills, fosters a growth mindset, and builds a foundation for sustained success and well-being.

ᐛᐛᐛ

"Reflecting on progress helps children learn from their experiences. Encouraging self-assessment fosters a growth mindset and continuous improvement. This practice builds self-awareness and a commitment to personal growth."

TWENTY-ONE
SUMMARY

In the journey of nurturing well-rounded, resilient, and capable children, various strategies and practices play a pivotal role. Each approach, from mindfulness to goal setting, and from family time to habit tracking, contributes significantly to a child's development. By integrating these practices into daily routines, parents and educators can foster essential skills and values, ensuring children grow into confident, empathetic, and successful individuals.

Mindfulness is a powerful practice that helps children develop calmness, focus, and emotional resilience. Teaching mindfulness involves incorporating simple techniques such as deep breathing, body scans, and mindful listening into daily routines. These practices help children become more aware of the present moment, manage their emotions, and enhance their concentration. Mindfulness also promotes empathy and self-awareness, enabling children to understand and share the feelings of others. Integrating mindfulness into daily activities, such as eating, movement, and creative expression, provides children with practical tools to navigate the challenges of life with a sense of peace and balance.

Reading together is another impactful activity that fosters a love for books, enhances literacy skills, and strengthens the bond between adult and child. Creating a welcoming reading environment, selecting engaging and appropriate books, and making reading a regular part of daily life can instill a lifelong appreciation for literature. Reading together not only improves cognitive abilities but also promotes emotional development, empathy, and imagination. Shared reading experiences provide opportunities for meaningful interactions, discussions, and reflections, reinforcing the importance of storytelling and the joy of reading.

Chores and family responsibilities teach children about responsibility and cooperation. Engaging children in household tasks provides practical lessons in accountability, teamwork, and the value of contributing to the family and community. Age-appropriate tasks, positive reinforcement, and a supportive environment make chore time an enjoyable and educational experience. Through chores, children develop essential life skills, such as organization, time management, and problem-solving. These skills contribute to their self-sufficiency and confidence, preparing them for independent living and future success.

Goal setting inspires ambition and achievement in children. By teaching children how to set and pursue meaningful goals, parents and educators can help them develop essential skills such as planning, perseverance, and self-discipline. Effective goal setting involves understanding the importance of goals, choosing appropriate and engaging targets, creating actionable plans, and maintaining motivation and focus. Through intentional guidance, positive reinforcement, and a supportive environment, children can cultivate a sense of purpose and direction, fostering personal growth and success. Goal setting also teaches children the value of effort and persistence, helping them navigate challenges with resilience and determination.

Time management and organizational skills are critical components of effective goal setting and personal development. By understanding the value of time, setting realistic schedules, and using tools and techniques to stay organized, children can build habits that support their productivity and well-being. Teaching prioritization, addressing procrastination, and fostering accountability are essential for effective time management. Balancing different aspects of life, modeling positive behaviors, and maintaining flexibility are key to creating a sustainable and fulfilling approach to managing time. Developing these skills helps children achieve a better balance between their responsibilities and personal interests, enhancing their overall quality of life.

Positive self-talk is a powerful tool for building confidence and resilience in children. By guiding children to use affirming and constructive language, parents and educators can help them develop a strong sense of self-worth and the ability to cope with challenges. Understanding the importance of positive self-talk, recognizing and replacing negative self-talk, practicing positive affirmations, and creating a supportive environment are essential steps in fostering these habits. Complementing positive self-talk with mindfulness practices, goal setting, and social support further enhances children's emotional well-being and resilience. Through intentional guidance and practice, children can develop the skills and mindset needed to navigate life's challenges with confidence and resilience.

Social skills are essential for fostering friendships and cooperation, playing a crucial role in a child's development and overall well-being. Developing strong social skills helps children build meaningful relationships, navigate social interactions, and work effectively with others. These skills encompass a range of behaviors, including communication, empathy, problem-solving, and cooperation. By nurturing these abilities, parents and educators can equip children with the tools they need to thrive in social settings and form lasting friendships. Creating supportive and inclusive environments, modeling positive behavior, and providing opportunities for practice and reflection are key strategies for promoting social skills development.

Gratitude practice is another powerful tool for nurturing appreciation and fostering a positive mindset in children. By helping children understand the concept of gratitude, incorporating it into daily routines, and creating opportunities for thankfulness, parents and educators can cultivate a habit of appreciation. Practices such as gratitude journaling, family rituals, acts of kindness, mindfulness, storytelling, and creative activities can all contribute to a deeper sense of gratitude. Addressing barriers to gratitude and providing a supportive environment further enhances the practice. Through consistent modeling, reflection, and authentic expression, children can develop a lifelong habit of gratitude that enhances their emotional well-being and overall happiness.

Creative expression is vital for encouraging artistic habits and providing children with a unique outlet for self-expression. Artistic activities such as drawing, painting, sculpture, music, dance, and drama allow children to communicate their thoughts, emotions, and ideas in ways that words may not always capture. Fostering creative expression helps children develop critical thinking, problem-solving skills, and emotional intelligence. It also promotes confidence, resilience, and a sense of accomplishment. By providing opportunities for exploration, creating a supportive environment, and integrating creativity into daily routines, parents and educators can help children cultivate a lifelong appreciation for the arts.

Problem-solving is an essential skill that plays a crucial role in developing critical thinking. It enables individuals to navigate challenges, make informed decisions, and innovate solutions. Teaching children problem-solving involves guiding them through the process of identifying and understanding the problem, generating potential solutions, evaluating and selecting the best solution, and implementing and reflecting on the outcome. By fostering these abilities, parents and educators can help children become confident, independent thinkers capable of addressing complex issues. Collaboration, communication, experiential learning, and technology integration further enhance these skills, providing opportunities for practical application and continuous growth.

Family time is a cornerstone of healthy relationships and personal well-being, playing a crucial role in strengthening bonds and creating lasting traditions. Engaging in shared activities, establishing rituals, and prioritizing meaningful interactions foster a sense of unity and connectedness among family members. By emphasizing the importance of family time, parents can instill values, build trust, and create cherished memories that last a lifetime. Creating a supportive environment, managing technology use, balancing family time with individual needs, and involving extended family members contribute to a positive and nurturing family environment. Through intentional effort and a commitment to spending quality time together, families can create a foundation of love, support, and resilience.

Habit tracking is a powerful and effective tool for celebrating progress and fostering personal growth. By identifying specific goals, selecting appropriate tracking methods, and maintaining consistency, individuals can develop positive habits and achieve their objectives. Celebrating small wins, reflecting on progress, and visualizing growth enhance motivation and reinforce positive behaviors. Accountability, both individual and collective, provides additional support and encouragement. Integrating habit tracking into daily routines, educational settings, and family activities creates a structured and supportive environment for personal development. Through intentional practice and mindfulness, habit tracking cultivates important life skills, fosters a growth mindset, and builds a foundation for sustained success and well-being.

In conclusion, the practices of mindfulness, reading together, engaging in chores, setting goals, managing time, practicing positive self-talk, developing social skills, nurturing gratitude, encouraging creative expression, solving problems, spending family time, and tracking habits are all integral to fostering well-rounded, resilient, and capable children. Each of these practices contributes to the development of essential skills and values, providing children with the tools they need to navigate the challenges of life with confidence and grace. By integrating these practices into daily routines, parents and educators can create a supportive and nurturing environment that promotes personal growth, emotional well-being, and overall happiness. The benefits of these practices extend far beyond childhood, providing a foundation for lifelong success and fulfillment. Through intentional guidance, support, and encouragement, children can develop the skills and mindset needed to thrive in all areas of life, building a brighter future for themselves and their communities.

Citation And References

This book represents the culmination of extensive research and meticulous analysis, incorporating a diverse range of sources, including numerous books, scholarly studies, and personal experiences. Additionally, I have scoured various websites to gather relevant information and data essential for the compilation of this work. I have taken every precaution to ensure the accuracy of the information presented and have diligently cited all sources to acknowledge their contributions.

Despite these efforts, the possibility of inadvertent errors remains. I deeply value the insights of my readers and appreciate any feedback that can help identify and rectify such inaccuracies. I encourage you to bring any discrepancies to my attention.

Your feedback is not only welcome but crucial, as it will aid in correcting current editions and enhancing the content of future ones. I am committed to maintaining the highest standards of accuracy and reliability in my work and thank you for your support and understanding.

Additionally, I firmly uphold the principle of freedom of speech and expression as guaranteed under Article 19(1)(a) of the Constitution of India, and I respect the diverse viewpoints and expressions of all readers.

PPP

Other Books Of The Author

1. Empowering Minds: A Journey into Women's Self-Discovery and Power
2. The Dynamics of Motivation: Catalyzing Thought into Action
3. Meditation and Mental Well Being: The Path to Inner Peace and Clarity
4. The Psychology of Child Education: Nurturing Future Generations
5. Ethical Enlightenment: A Modern Guide to Living with Integrity
6. Voices of Empowerment: Stories of Women Rising Against Odds
7. Social Psychology in Everyday Life: Understanding Human Connections
8. The Essence of Motivational Speaking: Inspiring Change in Others
9. Balancing Acts: Women, Work, and the Will to Lead
10. Guiding with Grace: Raising Children with Compassion and Awareness
11. The Power of Positive Aging: Embracing Life After Fifty
12. Building Resilient Communities: Social Work in Action
13. The Ethical Educator: Principles for Teaching and Learning
14. From Insight to Impact: Social Psychology for a Better World
15. The Ethics of Empathy: A Guide to Ethical Living
16. The Science of Empowering the Self: Navigating Life's Challenges with Psychological Wisdom
17. The Mindful Conscious Leader: Meditation Techniques for Modern Management
18. Pioneering Spirit: Women's Pathways to Leadership and Empowerment
19. Feeling to Healing: The Role of Emotional Intelligence in Child Development
20. Transformative Talks and Words of Inspiration: Insights into Motivational Oratory

21. Green Ethics: A Path to Sustainable Living
22. Spiritual Integrity: Navigating Life with Moral Compassion
23. Clean Living, Clean Society: The Ethics of Cleanliness
24. Patriotic Spirits: Building a Nation on Positive Attitudes
25. Innovative Integrity & Vibrant Visions: The Ethical and Entrepreneurial Spirit of Gujarat
26. Youthful Visions, Endless Possibilities: Inspiring Ethics and Motivation in Children
27. Living Your Legacy: How to Motivate Others by Living Your Values
28. Secret of Healing Conversations: Ethical Practices in Counselling and Therapy
29. Creative Kindness: Crafting a Life of Compassion and Creativity
30. The Power of Appreciation: How Gratitude Can Transform Your Relationships
31. Bhagavad-Gita: Messages
32. Science of Art: The New Frontier of Fashion Modernism
33. Vivekananda's Virtues: A Blueprint for Modern Living
34. Empower Her: Navigating the Path to Women's Entrepreneurship
35. The Boundless Classroom: Innovations in Global Education
36. The Language of Leadership: Communicating with Authenticity and Impact
37. The Warrior's Mantra: Deciphering the Hanuman Chalisa
38. Echoes of Empathy: Transformative Stories of Social Service
39. Artful Living: Cultivating Creativity in Your Daily Routine
40. Finding Your Why: Discovering Your Passions and Charting Your Course
41. The Role of Social Media in Shaping Self-Esteem and Interpersonal Relationships among Adolescents
42. Karma's Tapestry: Weaving a Life of Selfless Service
43. Altruistic Alchemy: Transforming Lives Through Giving
44. The Blueprint of Pro-Activeness and Productivity: Crafting Habits for Success
45. The Simplicity with Grounded Wisdom: Embracing Authenticity

in a Complex World

46. Secret of Solopreneur's Odyssey: Navigating the Path to Self-Employment
47. Exploring Tapestry of Peace: Global Perspectives on Harmony
48. The Art and Actions of Connection: Mastering Communication for Impact
49. She Governs and at the Helm: Strategies for Political Empowerment
50. Rising Above and Rising with Grace: A Woman's Roadmap to Career Mastery
51. The Effect of Networking & Connectedness: Building Strategic Alliances for Women
52. Beyond his Barriers: Women Thriving in Male-Dominated Fields
53. Secret of Inner Compass: Navigating Life with Intuition
54. Creative & Pro-Active Muses: A Celebration of Women in the Arts
55. Unburdened: The Art of Releasing the Past
56. Amplified Voices: Speeches of Women that Astonished the World
57. Secret of Manifesting Dreams: A Woman's Guide to Intentional Living
58. Ethics and Value Based Education: Reimagining Japan's School System
59. The Moral Compass Curriculum: A Holistic Approach
60. Tech with Heart: Integrating Ethics into Digital Learning
61. Honoring Virtue: Recognizing Ethical Excellence in Education
62. Raising Good Humans: A Guide to Character Development
63. The Spark Within: Nurturing Creativity in Children
64. The Teenager Whisperer: Navigating Adolescence with Grace
65. Igniting a Passion for Learning: Inspiring Lifelong Curiosity
66. The Habit Lab: Cultivating Positive Behaviors in Children
67. Seeds of Empathy: Fostering Compassion in Young Hearts
68. The Reading Revolution: Inspiring a Love of Books in Children
69. The Learning Brain: Unlocking the Secrets of Student Success
70. Teaching for All: Differentiated Instruction Strategies
71. The Time Alchemist: Mastering Time Management for Peak Performance

Bhajan

101. Pilgrimage of the Soul: Spiritual Journeys in India

❧❧❧

• 173 •

Contact

Dr. Minakshi Bansal
Social Activist
Ahmedabad, Gujarat, Bharat
minakshiindiag20@yahoo.com

ϷϷϷ

|| LOKAHA SAMASTHAHA SUKHINO BHAVANTU ||

9 7 9 8 8 9 4 4 6 9 0 8 9